IN THE
LIGHT
OF GOD'S LOVE

*Walking out of Brokenness
Into Wholeness*

LINDA D. BOLTON

*A True Story of God's Incredible
Love, Mercy and Grace*

IN THE LIGHT OF GOD'S LOVE
© Copyright 2003 by Linda Bolton

International Standard Book Number:
1-894928-34-2

Biblical References also taken from the
King James Version.

Printed in Canada

DEDICATION

This book is dedicated with love to my wonderful Heavenly Father who graciously sent His Son Jesus, my Saviour and Friend, and the Holy Spirit my Comforter and Counselor.

Without You this testimony would not be possible. Where would I be without Your love, forgiveness and redemption?

I also dedicate this story to the most incredible man in the universe—my lover, my best friend, my confidante, my co-heir in the kingdom, my husband Dale, (oh how I love you big muh) and to our four terrific children, Chad, Jason, Anna and Jeff.

You are the sunshine, you are the laughter, you give me reason to thank God every morning and to be on my knees every night. Come follow Jesus with me!

ACKNOWLEDGEMENTS

There are so many people who have loved and encouraged and inspired me throughout my life. I thank God every day for the wonderful parents He gave me; for the incredible example my mother has been, with her grateful and loving heart toward God and life. I couldn't have asked for a better Mom. I am thankful for a father who was honest, hard-working, and a real man of integrity. (He is now with Jesus)

My heart is blessed every day by the amazing family and friends that God has given us. Dale's parents are an inspiration to me. I am thankful for their love and acceptance. How grateful I am for my best girlfriend Sharon Coburn, who was so excited to see me finally write my story. How I praise God for her healing and her life message.

I am especially thankful for the love and support we share with our extended family at Thornhill Vineyard Christian Fellowship.

Special thanks to everyone who has been helpful in the completion of this book. Thank you to Ron Wilson and Michael Vallins for your editing, input and for encouraging me to press on toward the goal of finishing this book.

ENDORSEMENTS

This is a must read story, where after two failed marriages, an abortion, and numerous encounters with the hard knocks of life, Linda was able to find God's purpose for her life. This is a true testimony of how the Lord exchanges beauty for ashes and joy for mourning. I would encourage anyone who needs hope in the midst of despair to embrace the message of this book.

Carol Arnott,
Co Senior Pastor, Toronto Airport Christian Fellowship.

What a wonderful story of redemption! God's redeeming power is the "reason" for this testimony. To God be the glory; He is glorified in Linda's life. Her story has and will continue to touch many lives as they hear and read about what God has done in the midst of her life and circumstances. I know you will be encouraged and receive hope for yourself and others as you read of this amazing journey—which begins and ends with the unconditional love of God toward His beloved daughter Linda.

Muriel Bond

Linda's testimony is a beautiful example of how God can work through us. It shows that no matter what happens in our

ENDORSEMENTS

lives, the good, the bad, the hurts, the pains, that God will help us all the way. She gives us the example: be obedient and persevere, take God's truth to heart and it is possible; the truths become realities. Thank you Linda for giving us the hope and encouragement to develop what God has put into our lives so that we can make our own realities too.

Esther Cheng

Linda's story is a wonderful testimony of God restoring a broken life. In the process of editing this book I shared it with a couple of friends who were very much impacted by the reality of God's mercy and grace as demonstrated in Linda's experiences. For those who have suffered traumatic marriage breakdowns, it will be a great encouragement to find all the healing in God's love that they need in order to have healthy relationships.

Ron Wilson

CONTENTS

CONTENTS

FOREWORD

I have known my best friend Linda for almost twenty-four years. When I look back to the first time I met her I can hardly believe what God has done in her life. We met one evening at a clothing party at a friend's house. I had previously seen her, a beautiful blonde woman walking with her little boy on the beach and had mistaken her for some woman of privilege-(probably married to some rich doctor I thought.) I couldn't have been more wrong. Linda was a struggling young single mom trying to make ends meet by working three jobs and I had just started my business as an Independent Sales Director for Mary Kay cosmetics. We became instant friends and have traveled some perilous roads together. I particularly remember Linda and I going to a Christian Women's Club meeting where we heard a woman sharing about her struggle with cancer and how her husband had had an affair on her. I said to Linda, "I could never handle having cancer" and Linda said, "I could never handle a husband having an affair." We are both living proof, as to how God can give you the grace, courage and stamina to endure such trials.

As you read her story (we always laughed and said that no one would believe this could be non-fiction,) I pray that you will be as inspired as I was, and continue to be, by her spirit. Through the many trials that continued to attack Linda, I was always

FOREWORD

impressed by her fearless and tireless dependence on God. This is a true-life story of how God can bring victory and redemption out of a life of complete brokenness. It blesses me to watch how God has taken the ashes of Linda's life to use them to bring glory and honor to His name. Linda shares her story with humor, honesty and a humility that will astound you. I know that whoever reads this testimony will be continually amazed at God's great love, mercy and compassion. I believe that Linda's heart in sharing it, is to help other men and women to understand the reality of a God who loves, forgives and cares about every situation we go through in our lives. What a gift God has given to me in a true best girlfriend... a woman of substance and grace. May your hearts be touched as you read this incredible true story.

Sharon Coburn,
Senior Sales Director, Mary Kay Cosmetics,
100 Huntley Street guest.

INTRODUCTION

Where do I begin to tell the story of how God has taken a life totally shattered and broken and brought healing, redemption and wholeness? When I look back over the past twelve years it is nothing short of a miracle to discover how God has transformed me from an insecure, suicidal, and wounded woman into a person who knows at a heart level the awesome unconditional love and forgiveness of the Father.

The Lord asked me to write this book approximately seven years ago while ministering in Finland. It was there He gave me the title, *In the Light of God's Love*, and confirmed to me through many other prophetic words in Germany and England that I was to print my story. It is my belief and prayer that God will use the experiences that I share, to enlighten, and heal and encourage others who are going through the pain of rejection, divorce, abortion, and other forms of brokenness. I am not proud of some of the things I have done in my lifetime, but I am eternally thankful that I have a heavenly Father who loved me enough to send His Son to die for my sins.

The title, *In the Light of Gods Love*, was given to me by God, to help us realize the importance of not only seeing *life* in the light of His love, but to help us understand the reality of bringing everything of darkness or that which is secret, into the light. It is only when we are transparent before God and man that we can receive healing and inner peace. When we look at life's situations and other people through the light of God's love we will walk away with new vision and deeper understanding as to how much He loves and cares for each one of us.

I believe that it is God's heart that everyone who is walking in brokenness would come to that place of wholeness, as they understand their particular experience in the light of His love. That is my prayer — that God will use this story to bring glory and honor to Him and that it will help bring freedom to those who read it. May God bless you as you travel the road with me from brokenness to wholeness.

PART I

EARLY YEARS

CHAPTER 1

CAN ANYTHING GOOD COME FROM CABBAGETOWN?

For you created my inmost being; you knit me together in my mother's womb. I praise you because I am fearfully and wonderfully made; your works are wonderful, I know that full well.
Psalms 139: 13,14

I was born (at a very early age!) at St. Michael's Hospital in Toronto. When I was three months old, my parents moved into a small row house in the heart of the slums just east of Toronto's downtown core. Everyone still calls this area "Cabbagetown", even though it has been many years since farmers grew crops of cabbages there. As long as I can recall, I heard the saying, "Can anything good come from Cabbagetown?" I determined as a very little girl that my life would definitely prove that something good *could* come from there.

Even though growing up in Cabbagetown had some difficult times, I can honestly say that I have many happy childhood memories.

MY CATHOLIC EDUCATION

Being Roman Catholic, my parents sent my two sisters, my brother and I to a Catholic elementary school. I vividly remember my grade four teacher making us put our heads down on our desks just before going to confession. She would go through each of the Ten Commandments, asking us if we had committed any of them. We would always giggle when Miss Dudley asked us if we had committed adultery. We did not really know what it meant; one of the girls said it had to do with looking at dirty pictures or something like that.

On Monday mornings, Miss Dudley would ask those of us who had not gone to Mass on Sunday to stand up beside our desks and explain why not. I was horrified if I had missed Mass and felt so humiliated in front of the whole class. One Monday morning, I told my Mom that I did not want to go to school. When she asked my reason, I replied, "Because I didn't go to Mass on Sunday and Miss Dudley will make me stand up and tell the rest of the class." Mom stated that from now on I was not to stand up, because it was between God and me and none of my teacher's business.

Having developed an unhealthy fear of God based on teachings from my childhood. I perceived Him to be unkind and unloving. I imagined Him waiting for me to make a mistake and just ready to hit me over the head with a big stick. I believed that if I committed a sin and did not go to confession that I would either go to hell or, at best, purgatory.

Although I believed that Jesus was God's Son, I did not have a personal relationship with Him. I saw Jesus as a big white round host who came into me during communion and made my soul white. Then, if I sinned, I collected little black marks that eventually, if I sinned enough, would wipe Jesus out of my soul until I went to confession and communion again. It seemed like a vicious circle with no hope in sight.

DIXON HALL

Mrs. Fleury, Mrs. Dyer, and Mr. Abbit ran a wonderful Christian Community Club called Dixon Hall. It was sponsored by The United Way for the children of Cabbagetown. It was there that I memorized John 3:16:

For God so loved the world that he gave his one and only Son, that whoever believes in him shall not perish but have eternal life.

It was not until much later on in my life that I came to truly understand the personal significance of that scripture verse.

One of the things that I loved the most about Dixon Hall was that they made Christianity seem like fun. They helped me to see another side of God through the stories they told us about Jesus. We learned many wonderful Christian songs that I have since taught to my own children. I first learned how to folk dance at Dixon Hall. In addition, I would help out with the younger children with their arts and crafts and dancing. Some of the kids in the community would get angry at me and call me "Miss Goody Two Shoes" because I liked to help.

BORN TO ACT

From the time that I can remember, I always loved to be on stage. I used to sing and dance and make up plays for the kids in the neighbourhood to take part in. Of course, I always made sure that I played the lead role, seeing that I had produced, written, and directed them as well. Being in theatre and dancing was a love of mine from the time I was a very little girl. My mother tells me that, even while sitting on my potty, I still would sing and dance my way all around the room. The man living in the apartment below us would ask Mom who was making all the scratching noises on the floor.

BEATEN UP

As I grew into young adolescence, it seemed that the neighbourhood children were constantly beating me up, and either my big brother Mike or my little sister Debbie would come to my rescue. One day when I was 12 years old, a girl who was 15 made me kneel down in a mud puddle in the CBC parking lot and beg her not to beat me up in front of all my friends. I was so ashamed and humiliated that I made a vow that no one would ever hurt or humiliate me again.

DAD, MOM AND ME

My Dad seemed an unemotional type of person and had a difficult time showing love to us as children. He had experienced a great deal of emotional pain in his childhood due to the traumatic deaths of several of his brothers and sisters from sickness and accidents. His way of coping was to shut down his emotions, and thus he shut out those people that he loved the most. I knew deep in my heart that my Daddy really loved me but did not understand at that time why he had such a hard time showing affection to me. I so longed to be held in his arms that often I would pretend to be asleep in the car so he would have to carry me into the house. I loved to feel the warmth of his arms around me; they always felt so secure.

In response to my father's lack of affection, I became extremely performance oriented. I believed, in order for my earthly father or my Heavenly Father to love and accept me, I had to prove myself to them by being good and being a high achiever. I was probably one of the most goal-oriented 5-year-olds you could ever meet.

CAN ANYTHING GOOD
COME FROM CABBAGETOWN?

Dad was an alcoholic, although he would never have admitted it. He held down a good job most of his life; and, because his drinking never interfered with his work, he believed that he did not have a problem. Part of the frustration that my Mom had with him was the fact that they were always in debt, partially due to his drinking, and his desire to own brand new cars every two to three years. These factors explain why we had to live in the slums.

My childlike view of marriage and male-female relationships was marred by the fact that I saw my mother working hard all day long—keeping house, cooking, doing laundry and caring for us children—and then, in the evening, she would clean offices and washrooms at the Toronto City Hall to help make ends meet. It seemed that all my Mom did was work. I often heard her say, "It is a man's world!" I developed a root of bitterness at an early age, expecting that all women were slaves and men were the slave drivers.

I can remember asking God why he had made me a female and praying that I could be a boy instead of a girl. I certainly did not have a good attitude about being a woman. I got really ticked off as I grew up to discover that not only did women have to be slaves to men but that they had to endure menstrual cramps, PMS, and horrible pains during labour. I wished many times that God had made me a man. In recent years, I have repented for this spiritual rebellion, and now feel very positive about being a woman.

As a little girl, I can recall being upset because Mom usually worked the 3:00pm to 11:00pm shift, and I only got to see her first thing in the morning and on weekends. I would run home from school hoping to meet her on the street or catch a glimpse of her on the streetcar. Mom was always very loving and affectionate and was such a great encouragement and support to us kids that it helped to make up for the times she was not there. One of my favorite memories is the many times Mom took the time to play with us. She

IN THE LIGHT OF GOD'S LOVE

would play double dutch skipping, join us in a rousing game of touch football on the beach or go skinny dipping way out in the lake at Sauble Beach. Everyone would be shocked as my Mom, sisters and other friends and I would come out of the water with each other's bathing suits tops and bottoms on. What great fun we had.

I judged both my parents in different ways. I judged my Mom for not standing up to my Dad and also for her attitude towards men. In my Dad's case it was for his alcoholism and inability to be affectionate. I also judged him for always saying "No!" without giving us a reason; all he would say was: "Because I said 'No'!" If we wanted money, we would always have to go to Mom for a nickel because Dad's answer would be "No!" As a result I started to see my heavenly Father as someone who did not want to bless me.

MY SIBLINGS

I got along well with my three siblings most of the time, with the occasional fight thrown in for good measure. One of the fights that stands out most in my mind is the time that my older brother Mike was teasing me unmercifully (as usual!). I was playing "lady in the tight skirt", which means placing a rubber ball in a sock and swinging it back and forth across your body and between your legs and bouncing it off a wall. (Can you get the picture?) Anyway, this particular day, I put a 5-pound ball bearing of my father's in the sock and proceeded to hit my brother in the back of the head. (After all a girl can only take so much teasing!) My parents were very upset with me. Another time, as my brother Mike was teasing my older sister Pat, she poked him in the nose with her fork and drew blood. I do not know who you should have felt more sorry for—my brother or us girls! Debbie, being the youngest would scream blue murder whenever Mike would bug her. You could hear her bellows of sorrow all over the neighbourhood. People couldn't believe the size of her lungs, for such a wee lass.

8

CAN ANYTHING GOOD
COME FROM CABBAGETOWN?

Pat was the best big sister any girl could ask for. She was eight years older than I, but she never seemed to mind me tagging along with her. She would take me with her when she would meet her boyfriends and I always felt loved and accepted by her. She was an amazing swimmer and dancer and taught me all she knew in these areas. One time, just after she had obtained one of her first jobs, she threw a wonderful birthday party for me. She had the room all decorated and the table looked so fancy with place cards and everything. The highlight was the doll cake that she had specially made for me. I will never forget her kindness to me as a child.

My younger sister Debbie and I had our occasional scraps. She was really good at beating me up, but heaven help anyone else in the neighbourhood that picked a fight with me! She was always sticking up for me in front of the other kids. Mom used to say to me that if I did not fight back that she would hit me as well. Thank God, I had Debbie to fight my battles for me. Nonetheless, we all lived to tell the tale and have remained close all of our lives.

Christmas was particularly special for me. I knew that we celebrated Jesus birthday and was always in awe of that little babe in the manger and why He had to come and die on the cross. Mom and Dad tried to get us special gifts that we had asked for from Santa and I remember how devastated I was when my sister Debbie revealed to me that Santa was not real. Somehow it took the magic out of Christmas because I knew that Mom and Dad could not afford very much and I was hesitant to ask for too much after I knew the truth.

THE COTTAGE

Some of my favourite childhood memories were the times we spent at our small cottage on the Sauble River near Owen Sound, which my parents bought when I was 10. It was a great spot to have fun with friends. One time, Mom and Dad allowed me to invite 30 of the kids from our school musical production up to the cottage for a weekend cast party.

Sometimes, I would go with my mother into Owen Sound to shop. On one of those shopping trips, when I was twelve years old, I told my mother that I was going to live in Owen Sound someday. Sure enough, my words did come true; however, I could never have imagined what I eventually did experience in that city.

CHAPTER 2

MY TEEN YEARS

Since my youth, O God, you have taught me, and
to this day I declare your marvelous deeds.
Psalm 71:17

J ust prior to high school, I decided to change my name from
Linda to Lynn because I did not like my name and did not
like who I was. Since a girl in my grade eight class named
Lynn had been very popular, I thought it would help my popular-
ity if I was called Lynn, too. Every time someone called me
Linda, I would get upset and declare indignantly, "My name is
Lynn!" Both of my parents were disturbed with my decision;
however, in my teenage rebellion, their feelings did not seem to
matter to me.

Also, just prior to high school, I decided not to go to church
any more. I would pray to God when I needed help or when I was
very thankful for something special, but I seemed to lose interest
in Him for the next several years.

HIGH SCHOOL

My favourite years were between the ages of 14 and 19. These high school years were truly wonderful. I chose to attend Central Technical High School since I had decided as a child that I wanted to be an artist. Moreover, I thought it was great that the school was located on the other side of Toronto, because I figured no one would be able to discover that I came from Cabbagetown.

During my first year at Central Tech, my brother took me to see one of the Broadway musicals that the school put on every year. I was hooked. The next year, I tried out for a part in *Gentlemen Prefer Blondes* and got the second lead role of Jane Russell. From that point on, my artwork was put aside. I soon had to decide between art and drama; so I chose to stay in the plays. The following year, I entered the Registered Nursing Assistant Course (RNA) offered there at Central Tech.

Besides playing a lead role in four musicals, I was a cheerleader and on the school's social committee. Furthermore, I was awarded the title of Miss Centech 1971 and chosen to represent my school in the Young Voyagers program in British Columbia. The year after I left, I was asked to come back to receive the first K. E. Chute Memorial Award; he had been the principal during my years at Central Tech and had died during my final year there. This award was given to the student or students who made extraordinary contributions in extracurricular activities.

On my last day at Central Tech, I stood on the steps of the school and cried my eyes out. I did not want to say goodbye to the wonderful times that I had experienced there and the friends that I had made.

When I graduated as an RNA, I decided to do what my mother had wanted — to go on for my R.N. at the Credit Valley School of Nursing in Mississauga, instead of going to the Academy of Fine Arts in New York. I have never regretted that decision.

MY PARENTS' DIVORCE

Although my teen years were mostly happy, I was troubled at the growing tension between my parents that ended in a divorce when I was sixteen. When Mom first threatened to leave Dad after being married over 25 years, she told him she would stay if he sought help for his drinking. But he refused.

I judged my parents for getting a divorce. I am ashamed to admit it, "but I frequently judged people who had been divorced with a self-righteous attitude." I would say things like, "What's wrong with them that they can't stay married?" I guess I thought that divorce was just an easy way out of a difficult situation.

For me the saddest result of my parent's divorce was their decision to sell the cottage. I cried a million tears that year.

Five years later, my mother married Bill. At first, my dad was quite angry and jealous, but as the years went by, my stepfather Bill and my dad became very good friends. During the last years of their lives, they spent many hours together golfing and playing bridge and going to garage sales with Mom. I was very blessed by the way my dad, my step-dad and my mom were able to be blind to their differences and enjoy a very unusual, but precious, friendship. They were a fine example of how forgiveness and letting go of bitterness can enhance one's life and the lives of those around them.

PART II

TWO PROBLEM MARRIAGES AND GOD'S SALVATION

CHAPTER 3

FIRST MARRIAGE

If we confess our sins, he is faithful and just and will
forgive us our sins and purify us from all unrighteousness.
1 John 1:9

"But I will restore you to health and heal your wounds,"
declares the LORD, "because you are called an outcast,
Zion for whom no one cares."
Jeremiah 30:17

Before my parents sold the cottage, I met my future husband at a dance at Sauble Beach. I was only sixteen years old. During the five years I went out with Tom, I tried several times to break off the relationship. I realized that he had a drinking problem, but I continued to date Tom because I felt sorry for him and loved his parents so much. I also had a co-dependent type of personality at that time that caused me to have a "saviour" mentality. I thought that somehow, if I married him, his drinking would decrease and we would live happily ever after. I was soon to discover that this was not the case. In fact, the longer we were married the worse the drinking problem became.

After being married two years, we had a son who we named Chad. In training as a nurse I had looked after patients who had caesarean sections when they had their babies. I was terribly afraid of having to have one and stated more than once,"I never want to have a C-section. That was exactly what happened to me. After I had been in labour for several hours they discovered that the baby was not coming and they had to do a c-section. After it was over I was laying on the stretcher in recovery and Tom came in to tell me that we had a beautiful son. I was in so much pain and was so upset about having had a c-section that I blurted out, "Oh, a son, good, I wouldn't want to bring a girl into this mans world". Then to add to my difficulties Chad ended up having colic. He cried all day and all night for three full months. Thank God, once he got over the colic he was the most easy-going toddler and child I have ever seen. His teachers wrote in his report card each year, "It is a pleasure to have Chad in my classroom". When Chad was 7 months old we took a trip to Jamaica together and had a great time, Tom brought home a large bottle of 110 proof rum. [He got very drunk approximately one month later and physically abused me.] He was a very insecure person, (perhaps because I had broken off with him so many times when we were dating) and would go into fits of jealous rage if a man even looked at me on the street. I told him that I could never live with that abuse and said he had to leave. Tom walked out of his son's life. Chad has seen his father only a few times since then. Tom was in many ways a good person. I have wondered what life would have been like had I stayed with Tom or if I had been a Christian then. However, I have learned that God does not want us to look back with regrets. He wants us to learn from our failures and allow Him to glorify himself in us as we learn to rely on Him. During the next couple of years, I had a few very hurtful relationships with men and was badly wounded as a result of them. I started recognizing that my life was a mess and that I was not doing a very good job of managing it on my own.

In preceding years, I had started taking an interest in spiritual things, such as getting involved in the Bahai Faith during my second year at Nursing School. I thank God that I recognized that their teachings about Jesus just being another prophet from God were not right. Nonetheless, I had a real desire to get to know God at a deeper level.

MEETING CHRISTIANS

After I broke up with Tom, God began to bring Christians across my path. When I was working as a head nurse in a nursing home in Owen Sound, I noticed that there was one housekeeping staff member who was different. She had a radiance about her as she "cleaned toilets unto the Lord". For Heddy, her work was a form of worship to the Lord. She had such a lovely countenance and always seemed to radiate joy and peace. Heddy was especially kind to the seniors in that place and they all loved her.

A couple of Christian nurses would invite me for a meal and would always pray before they ate. They were extremely eager to answer my questions about God, even when I was argumentative.

Probably the person that had the greatest influence in my accepting the Gospel was the Medical Advisor who visited the nursing home every Friday and did rounds with me. This doctor was a pleasant man, who had a very nice way with the seniors. He also had a determination that I was going to come to that place of knowing the truth about salvation. We would have some rather deep conversations. It did not matter how many difficult questions I would fire at him; he always had a good answer and never grew impatient with me. How thankful I am for this wonderful man of God!

During this time, I also started attending the Christian Women's club and came to understand about the salvation prayer that you must say in order to be "born again". Initially, I was very perplexed. How could a person go back inside their mother and be born again? I understood how Nicodemus felt! I finally came to realize that the spiritual part of me that communes with God had died with Adam and that I needed to be born again spiritually.

SALVATION

On Sept 13, 1980, I knelt down alone beside my bed and repented for the fact that I was a sinner and that I was making a mess of my life; I asked Jesus to come into my heart and take over the controls of my life. I really did not feel anything different that night. The next morning, however, while driving to my first day teaching a Health Care Aide Course in Lion's Head, I was filled with the Holy Spirit. I was praying and asking God to help me as I was very nervous about meeting my new class. I felt all warm and kind of "giddy" and this incredible peace and joy filled my heart. The very first thing I did was to tell all my students in the Health Care Aide course that I had just become a Christian and that they should, too! What a wonderful time I had with those twenty-two ladies, as I taught them about working with seniors and shared my newly discovered faith!

AN OUTCAST AND A DISCIPLE

When I first became a Christian, I concluded that I needed to attend church and so started going to an Evangelical church. They believed in the Holy Spirit but did not believe that the gifts of the Spirit were for today. They also struggled a great deal with the whole issue of divorce and remarriage. Further more, women with strong leadership personalities were not looked on favourably by some people in the church. In many ways, I started to feel more like a sinner and an outcast in the Christian community than I had in the world.

I can remember the pastor's wife, whom I loved and had an

excellent relationship with, telling me that because of my divorced status, I would have to prove myself to the people in the church. Since I was so performance oriented, I immediately set out to prove to the people in that church that I was just as saved as they were. I joined the choir, sang solos, taught Sunday school and Pioneer Girls, and was a leader in the College and Career group.

I look back on those years and realize now that all my work was hay, wood, and stubble before the Lord, because I could not accept that Christ's death on the Cross was payment enough to take away all of my sins. I understand now, that all my works are as filthy rags before the Lord because of the attitude in which I did them, and that "it is by grace that I have been saved not by works lest no man should boast". It took me several years to come to that place of understanding these truths in my heart.

DISCIPLED

In spite of these problems, the first years of my Christian walk were truly remarkable. The church assigned an elderly lady to disciple me; it was through Evelyn that I came to understand the importance of reading God's word. I was amazed how much I wanted to read the Bible. I would read it every chance I got. I kept it at the table with me during my meals and took it to work so that I could read it on my breaks. I just could not get enough of God's word. The Holy Spirit was bringing it to life for me and I understood it in a way that I had never been able to before.

"FEAR NOT FOR I AM WITH YOU"

I remember one particular incident when I had been asked to go and sing at the Barrie jail. I was really nervous about going there. I knew that I would be in an open room with several of the inmates and I was afraid for my safety. The night before we were to go, I was praying and asking God if I was doing the right thing. I told him that I was afraid and asked Him to let me know if I was

21

in His will.

The next morning I woke up and the Lord told me to turn to Jeremiah 1. When I opened up my Bible, I read the following:

> *"Ah, Sovereign LORD," I said, "I do not know how to speak; I am only a child. But the LORD said to me, "Do not say, 'I am only a child.' You must go to everyone I send you to and say whatever I command you. Do not be afraid of them, for I am with you and will rescue you,"* declares the LORD.* Jeremiah 1:6-8

After reading this passage I knew in my heart that God would be with me. I was filled with such incredible peace. I was able to go and minister at the jail and some of the prisoners came to know Jesus that day. HALLELUJAH!

CHAPTER 4

THE $16,000 HOUSE

*Bring the whole tithe into the storehouse, that there
may be food in my house. Test me in this," says the
LORD Almighty, "and see if I will not throw open the
floodgates of heaven and pour out so much blessing
that you will not have room enough for it.*
Malachi 3:10

I had so many answers to prayer during those wonderful first
years as a Christian!

GOD'S VOICE VS. RULES

As a new Christian I remember asking the Lord to show me
things that I was doing that were not in His will. Many of my new
Christian friends said that things like dancing, playing cards, and
going to movies were sinful. I had grown up enjoying these activities and could not understand why they were considered sinful,
nor could I find anything in the Bible that stated that they were
wrong.

Instead of following their set of rules, I decided to ask God to convict me whenever I did something that was not pleasing to Him; I developed a very sensitive spirit to knowing His will for my life. He has never to this day convicted me that dancing or card playing or watching certain movies are wrong for me. For some people, (i.e. those who have trouble in the area of immorality), dancing with members of the opposite sex may be wrong for them. We must always be open to what God is speaking to us as individuals.

TITHING

One of the first things the Lord did convict me about was the need to tithe. The Lord showed me that I was, firstly, stealing from Him and the storehouse by not tithing; and, secondly, I was robbing myself of the blessings that God had for me.

At that time, I was really struggling financially. As a single Mom, who was not receiving any support for my young son, I was working three jobs in order to make ends meet; and I was still having trouble keeping up with the bills. I did not know how I could afford to give up 10 percent of my income. However, I decided, in order to be obedient, I would have to step out in faith and give back to God a tenth of what He had given me.

After I started to tithe, I immediately noticed that I was always able to pay my bills and have food on the table. Within three months of my commencing to tithe, the Lord radically changed my financial picture. The first thing He did was open up the door for me to become the Director of Nursing at the facility that I had been working at for six years. Being able to make more money working one job and no longer having to work evenings or weekends, I was able to spend more time with my little boy at home.

A HOUSE FROM GOD

As a result of leaving the R.N. union when I became the

Director of Nursing, I was given a retroactive cheque worth $3000. My small two-bedroom apartment was quite adequate; however, I had been praying for some time that I would be able to buy a house instead of paying rent. I put the $3000 into the bank and started on my journey to find a house — one I could afford and I knew God already had picked out for me. I told the Lord that whatever house He gave me would be His house and that I would use the house to help others and bring honour to His name.

The first house I found was worth $36,000. I prayed and asked God to show me if this was the right house. I told Him that I would not be disappointed if I did not get it; I wanted the house that He had for me. The offer that I had put in fell through.

The next house I put an offer in on was for $26,000. I could not believe how nice it was for that amount of money and really prayed hard to God hoping that this was the right house for me. Again the offer fell through. I remember thinking that there was no way that I could find a cheaper house than that. Nevertheless, I knew that God had His hand on my life and that I had to trust Him with this.

Once again I set out to find the perfect house, the one I knew the Lord had for me. One day, as the real estate lady and I were driving down the street, I was looking through her book that had homes in it and came across a house that was listed for $19,900. "What about this house, Ruth?" I asked.

"That house has been empty for a year," she answered, "and is a real mess!" It had been a mortgage foreclosure and no one had been able to buy it.

When we drove up to it, we were looking at the saddest, ugliest house in the neighbourhood; obviously, it had not been looked after for a long, long time. The weeds were waist high in the front lawn. Divided into a duplex, it had two ugly front doors. Two dilapidated front steps were almost falling off. But strangely, in

IN THE LIGHT OF GOD'S LOVE

spite of all that, my heart immediately started pounding.

As Ruth entered the front door she turned back to me and exclaimed, "Oh, Lynn! It stinks in here. I don't think you want to go in here."

But I insisted. As we walked into the downstairs one-bedroom apartment, the Lord started showing me how the house could be put back into a single family dwelling by making some minor changes. The Lord spoke to me within minutes of being inside the house and He said to me in what I believe was an audible voice, "Offer $16,000."

I said to Ruth, "Has there been an offer on this place recently?"

"There was an offer for $18,000 three months ago, but C.M.H.C. would not accept it."

"I'm going to offer $16,000, because that's just what the Lord told me to offer." She looked at me as if I had two heads, but she wrote up the offer. Within a couple of days, I found out that they had accepted it. No one could believe it.

As time went by, I was able to move into the house and pay less for mortgage payments than I had been paying for rent. Moreover, I was even able to procure free government grant money for all the renovating I wanted to do! The government was offering these grants at that time for fixing up homes in the neighbourhood that were "eyesores". God knew how much this lovely home needed some tender loving care. With the grant money, I was able to put on a new roof, install a picture window to replace one of the front doors, put in a small driveway, replace the eavestroughing, paint the whole outside of the house, and add decorative shutters on the windows and doors. Inside, I was able to replace the carpets and flooring in the kitchen and bathroom. I put a new sundeck in the backyard.

On my first day in that house, I put a picture of my Jesus on

26

the wall and dedicated that home to Him. For the three years that I lived in that home, it was a haven of rest and encouragement to Chad and me and to many other people. How I praise God for the time spent in that house on Fourth Ave East!

When I sold the house three years later, I was able to clear $30,000. Our God more than amply supplies all of our needs!

CHAPTER 5

"ANGELS I HAVE HEARD ON HIGH"

For he will command his angels concerning you to
guard you in all your ways; they will lift you up in their
hands, so that you will not strike your foot against a stone.
Psalm 91:11,12

Soon after moving into my new home, I started attending Shallow Lake United Church occasionally. One Wednesday evening, I became very upset during a movie they were showing on the family. Upon hearing that children raised in single-parent homes often become gay or delinquent, I started to cry uncontrollably. When Larry Marshall, the pastor, came to me and asked me why I was crying, I told him that I was concerned about raising my little boy alone and what might happen to him. He asked several other people to come and pray for me.

While they were praying, I could feel a warm sensation flow from the top of my head to the bottom of my feet. I went from having uncontrollable sobbing to feeling incredible joy and laughter coming up from the inside of my abdomen. After they finished praying, I waited for a few minutes, bathing in God's wonderful presence, and then went out to my car to go home.

As soon as I turned on the ignition of my old beat-up station wagon, I immediately heard the most amazing singing that I had ever heard in my life. I knew beyond a shadow of a doubt that what I was audibly hearing was the heavenly host singing. All during that 30 minute ride back to Owen Sound, the angels continued to sing and worship God. As they sang, the Lord showed me sins I had committed as a little girl that I needed to repent for. In addition, He confirmed to me that "He would be a husband to the widow and a father to the fatherless". It says in Psa 68:5, "A father to the fatherless, a defender of widows, is God in his holy dwelling." He brought incredible peace into my heart concerning my little boy Chad. It was truly the best time that I have ever experienced in God's presence.

When I reached my home, I sat out in the car for the longest time. I did not want the worship to end, but eventually I had to let the babysitter go home. The first thing I did when I went into the house was to call a friend of mine who went to the church that I regularly attended. I told him about my experience hearing the angels and he responded by saying, "Oh, it must have been the radio." I knew it was not the radio because the radio station in Owen Sound had commercials every three minutes and they usually play Country and Western music.

The more I shared my story about hearing the angels worshipping, the more people thought I was hallucinating. As I said before, this church that I was attending did not believe in the gifts of the Holy Spirit for today. They believed that they were only for the apostolic days and did not believe in prophecy or speaking in tongues. I went through some confusing and difficult times during these years because I was hearing God's voice fairly frequently and sometimes I would hear even His audible voice.

WITNESSING

Over the next couple of years, I grew in relationship with Jesus and loved to share about my Saviour with anyone who would listen. It was during this time that I probably drove my poor family crazy. I was always telling them about the fact that if they did not accept Jesus that they were going to go to hell. I was pretty fanatical, but I also loved my parents and brother and sisters so much that I did not want them to miss out on this wonderful friend that I had found in Jesus. God truly blessed me when I was able to witness to my mother and as a result I saw her come to accept Jesus as her Lord and Saviour. It has really been a gift to have my mother as a sister in Christ.

CHAPTER 6

TO REMARRY OR NOT TO REMARRY, THAT IS THE QUESTION!

This is what the LORD Almighty says: "Administer true justice; show mercy and compassion to one another."
Zachariah 7:9

O ver the four years that I had been a Christian, I would ask the Lord from time to time about the possibility of remarrying. I searched the Scriptures and was often confused about the whole issue of remarriage. I had attended some Bill Gothard seminars that taught against remarriage, and yet I could not believe that God would intend for all divorced people to be alone the rest of their lives. I believed that God deals with people as individuals. I could not understand why divorce was the only sin not totally forgiven through Christ's death on the cross. It seemed that the church believed there were consequences that went along with being divorced that I was really having a hard time with; and so I earnestly sought the Lord.

After a time I felt released in my spirit to consider the possibility of remarriage, and the Church during that time seemed to be reconsidering the issue. New books were being written on the subject and God was giving more revelation to learned men and women in Christian circles. I dated off and on during this time and ended up in a couple of relationships where I either got hurt or ended up hurting some of the men I dated. For this I have asked forgiveness from them and from God.

MEETING JOHN

At the end of 1983, I met a man who had been dating one of the girls in our College and Career group, but he told me that he was no longer going out with her. John was a very attractive man, who was down on life and seemed very impressed with my walk with God. He could not believe how together I was for someone who had been divorced. Once again my co-dependent personality kicked into play and I thought that here was someone who needed me; here was someone I could help.

At first everything went well. He had two beautiful little boys—Michael was three and James, five. Chad, who was six at the time, thought it was just wonderful to have two new playmates. Chad had not seen his father for several years and had been praying that God would bring him a Daddy.

After dating for approximately six weeks, we became engaged. At the time, I really did not ask God if the man I was dating was the right one. I let my heart rule on what was best for me.

WEDDING PLANS MESSED UP

Shortly after, we ended up sleeping together. I was devastated. I knew that sex outside of marriage was sin. We had set a wedding date for May 13 and had all of the arrangements including our honeymoon paid for.

TO REMARRY OR NOT TO REMARRY, THAT IS THE QUESTION!

Two weeks prior to the wedding, John's first wife went to our pastor and told him that we were sleeping together. He confronted John about this, but he totally denied any sexual involvement with me. Then the pastor and his wife came out to my parents' place at Keppel and asked me the same question in front of my parents. I refused to answer the question, which told them that we were guilty.

We decided to postpone the wedding, and I went on our two-week honeymoon cruise with my son instead. While I was away, I determined that I would break off the relationship when I got home. However, I just could not seem to break away from the hold John had on my heart.

Over the next few months, we set two more dates to get married, but each time our plans fell through. Several people tried to tell me that I was not supposed to marry him. One woman who did not know me very well called me up one day and asked me to meet her at the A & W. She did not know why God had chosen her to give me this message, but all she knew was that she had to be obedient to what God had asked her to do. Then she shared with me that God told her to tell me that I was not to marry John.

I was so confused and did not know how I could get out of the relationship.

CHAPTER 7

OCTOBER 11, 1984

Surely the arm of the LORD is not too short to save,
nor his ear too dull to hear. But your iniquities have
separated you from your God; your sins have hidden his
face from you, so that he will not hear.
Isaiah 59:1,2

J ust when I felt that I might be able to end my relationship with John, I found out I was pregnant. I immediately told John, but he declared that he would not marry me. He flew into a rage and said that it would never work and that there was no way that he would marry me for that reason. I went home that night and cried myself to sleep.

I did not know what to do. Feeling totally cut off from God, I was not hearing his voice any longer and it seemed that I was falling deeper and deeper into a pit of despair. I was so worried that someone in that small town would find out that I was pregnant. Being so performance oriented, I was so afraid of what people would think of me. I had earned a very good reputation in my church and in the nursing home that I was working in. Most of all, I was so ashamed that I had let God down.

ABORTION

I came to a point of being in such over whelming darkness that I believed that the only thing that I could do was to have an abortion.

In nursing school, I had judged women having abortions with a self-righteous attitude. I swore I would never have an abortion, no matter what. Although I knew that it was murder, I went ahead, anyway.

On October 11, 1984, I drove down to a hospital in Toronto to have the abortion. While seeing the doctor, I could not help crying. All the way to the O.R., I was weeping and kept asking God and my unborn child to forgive me. Three times while in the waiting room, I got up to leave and then decided against it. It was the worst day of my life.

When it was over, I felt nothing for the first few days. I was numb. John could not believe that I had gone through with it. He had called me at the last moment to say that he would marry me, but I had made up my mind not to.

After being home for a few days, the realization of what I had done hit me with a vengeance. I spent many long days and nights crying and begging God for forgiveness. But I could not forgive myself.

MARRIAGE — PROBLEMS

As the weeks went on, John again started to bug me about marrying him. I finally decided to agree out of the guilt that I was feeling. I thought that somehow I could make it up to him or to our unborn child or something. I was not thinking logically. I felt like something had taken over the control of my will since I had first had sex with John and I was no longer acting out of my own free will.

To add to my sin, I ended up marrying John six weeks after I had the abortion, and things went from bad to worse. We were only married a couple of weeks when I found out that I was pregnant again. Initially I was happy, but felt that it was too soon into our marriage. Within six weeks I ended up having a miscarriage. I was upset because I felt that God was punishing me for what I had done.

During the first six months of our marriage, life was hell for both of us. Neither one of us could forgive the other for what had happened. All we did was argue and I would end up crying.

After we had been married approximately eight months, I had another miscarriage. This time I was very upset. I really wanted more children and once again my fear was that God was getting back at me for the abortion.

On October 11, one year after my abortion, I went into an inconsolable depression that lasted for several days. The slightest thing would remind me of what I had done. Every time I saw a picture of a baby I would cry. Every time I heard advertisements about abortions and the Right to Life, I would almost be sick to my stomach. It seemed that I could not get away from the pain.

JEFFREY'S BIRTH

When we had been married over two years, I gave birth to a beautiful baby boy, who we named Jeffrey, which means "God's peace". After he was born, our marriage started to get better. We had four wonderful boys who were closer to each other than full brothers. John had adopted Chad by this time and Chad just loved his new family. I loved Michael and James like they were my own children and spent many happy hours taking them to baseball and soccer games and playing with them on the farm. We were doing very well financially, and we were ministering together at our church. I really started to believe that things were going to work out for us. I had used the $30,000 from the sale of my $16,000 house to renovate John's old farmhouse and it looked amazing. The farm was situated on 350 acres. As well as raising cattle we also owned a number of horses and helped my father in law with his sleigh-ride and hay ride business. Life was ideal in many ways and I started to believe that God could make something good out of what the enemy had intended for evil.

It was around this time that the Lord showed me why I had never been able to receive healing and forgiveness for the abortion. I was so afraid of someone finding out about it, that I had never been able to confess it in front of a pastor. Shortly after this, I went to our minister and told him what had happened, and finally started to believe that maybe I could be forgiven.

But every year on October 11th I would go into a depression that would last for days. I just could not forgive myself for what I had done.

CHAPTER 8

"I COULD NEVER HANDLE A HUSBAND HAVING AN AFFAIR!"

"The LORD will call you back as if you were a wife deserted and distressed in spirit—a wife who married young, only to be rejected," says your God. "For a brief moment I abandoned you, but with deep compassion I will bring you back. In a surge of anger I hid my face from you for a moment, but with everlasting kindness I will have compassion on you," says the LORD your Redeemer.
Isaiah 54:6-8

Just around our fourth anniversary, I noticed a dramatic change in how my husband was relating to me. We had planned a special anniversary weekend away together at Fern Resort and the whole weekend John appeared distant, pre-occupied and argumentative. After that weekend he stopped being affectionate and always found an excuse to be out. Something was terribly wrong in our relationship, but I could not find out what it was. Over the next several months, I tried several times to persuade John to get counseling — without success. I became so depressed that I took a month's leave of absence from my work.

SHOTGUN AFFAIR

On February 9, 1990, John received a call from "one of our tenants" and as usual, he said he had to go out.

Around 8 p.m. he returned home. I was in the bathtub reading *No Compromise*, the story of Keith Green. He ordered me to get out of the tub and to get the children out of the house. I noticed that he had tears in his eyes and seemed upset.

"We live way out in the country," I objected. "Why do you want me to get the kids out of here, and where do you think that they are supposed to go?" He then told me to just shut them upstairs in their room. Chad, who was 12 at the time, had invited a friend to stay for the night and was very upset and embarrassed by what was happening.

After putting the children into one of the upstairs bedrooms, I went downstairs and discovered that John had loaded a shotgun. He proceeded to tell me to call the Pastor and ask him to come out to the farm. He then locked himself in the downstairs bathroom and told me that he had sinned against God and me, but that he would not tell me what he had done until the Pastor came. Frantically, I tried to call the Pastor. It took around 20 minutes to locate him at a friend's house.

When the pastor and his wife arrived at our home 15 minutes later, John came out of his hiding place. He then shared with us that he had started having an affair with an 18-year old girl shortly after she had moved into one of our apartment buildings.

I cannot begin to describe how I felt at that moment. I felt like I had been kicked in the gut. My heart was pounding and my mouth was dry and I did not know how to respond. I kept crying out to God, What should I do, what should I do?"

Within a few minutes, there was a knock at the door. His girl-friend was standing there asking John to come out and talk to her. Apparently, she had given him the ultimatum earlier in the evening that if he did not tell me about them, then she would.

He went outside with Kathy while still holding onto the gun. The pastor, his wife and I stayed in the house and prayed. I felt a tremendous peace come over me, and the Lord told me that I was to go outside and tell Kathy to leave the property, that I loved my husband, and that we were going to work things out. When I did this she still refused to leave and kept arguing with John about the gun.

After several more minutes, she finally left and John came back into the house. At that point, I was able to tell him that I would not leave him and that we would get counseling and get some help. He agreed to unload the shotgun and we collapsed in a heap on the floor, crying and talking quietly.

The pastor went outside to get a flask of oil from his car to anoint us. After what seemed a very long time, his wife decided to see what was taking him so long.

All of a sudden, the front door flew open, and we were sur-rounded by police. John's girlfriend had contacted the police, claiming that John was holding hostages at gunpoint. Needless to say, we were totally shocked and it took some time to convince the police of the truth. John was charged with unlawful use of a firearm and taken to the psychiatric unit of the hospital overnight because he had threatened suicide.

After they all left, I felt numb. I could not believe what had happened. I settled the children down, and then called my best friend Sharon. Even though Sharon had been diagnosed with can-cer a year before and had been dealing with her own pain, she and her husband Jim quickly came out to console me.

After sleeping very little that night, I awoke in the morning, feeling as if I was going to be physically sick. John phoned me from the hospital and asked me to come up and see him. My brother and sister came up to Owen Sound to be with me, and my father came over to look after the children for me.

As I drove up to the hospital, I kept asking God how was I ever going to be able to get through all this. He reminded me of the time when Sharon and I had been at a ladies meeting listening to a women share her experiences regarding her husband having an affair on her and dealing with life-threatening cancer. Sharon and I looked at each other and she said, "I could never handle having cancer". I said I could never handle a husband having an affair on me! Now I was about to see how God would get me through this.

The pastor and his wife came within a few minutes of my arrival in John's hospital room. They anointed us with oil and I felt the presence of God in a way that I had never felt before. God put such love and forgiveness in my heart for my husband that I could not believe it. That afternoon they discharged John, and we went home to see if we could turn our messed up lives around.

Over the next few weeks, we sought counseling, went on a trip to Florida, and even went to a Marriage Encounter weekend. My prayer was that we could work things out and keep our family together.

CHAPTER 9

MOVE TO CAMBRIDGE

*"Forget the former things; do not dwell on the past. See,
I am doing a new thing! Now it springs up; do you not
perceive it? I am making a way in the desert and
streams in the wasteland*
Isaiah 43:18,19

Approximately one month after I had found out about John's affair, I discovered that the position of Nursing Consultant at my company's head office in Cambridge was available. I asked John what he thought about my applying for it and he said, "Sure, it might be good for us to start over."

I was interviewed for the job and was offered it. John felt that I should take it. He said that we could keep our farm and sell our other properties. Accepting the position, I started April 1st and started to commute between Cambridge and Owen Sound with the intent of moving down to Cambridge when the school year was over.

We put an offer in on a suitable house in Cambridge. However, the day that the house was to close, I found out that

John had never stopped seeing his girlfriend since the first day he got out of the hospital and that he had bought a house with her in Wiarton (a little town near Owen Sound).

Furthermore, now I was stuck with this house that I could not afford to pay for on my own. I was not able to get out of the offer that we had put in on it, and I needed $37,000 to complete the deal. John refused to help me and so my wonderful mother, sister, and brother came up with the money so that I would be able to get the house.

The day we moved into that house in Cambridge was probably one of the saddest days of my life. I kept breaking down and weeping and trying to cope with how I was supposed to set up a new house, work an extremely stressful job, and try to deal with the realization that I had left my family, friends, and everything that had meant anything to me back in Owen Sound.

The first couple of months in Cambridge were very lonely. My children started going to a Christian school across the road, and so I decided that we would go to church there on Sundays as well. I would go and sit in the pew and cry all during the service, but no one would come and console me. I realize now that they probably just did not know how to deal with someone who was going through so much grief. But I so badly needed someone to cry with.

BACK WITH JOHN

A few weeks after John had walked away from his responsibility with the house, he started talking to me about taking him back. He told me that the affair with Kathy was over and that he had taken her name off the house they had bought. Because I was so lonesome, because I was missing my stepsons, because I felt that I was a total failure, and because I believed in forgiveness, I decided to try to work things out.

After the second time I had taken John back, the Lord had specifically told me through a prophetic word and through scripture that I was not to do so. The Lord said that I was prostituting myself before Him. He told me that I was to forget the former things and that He would restore the years that the locust had eaten; but I was still so confused and so broken that I kept walking in disobedience to what God was saying to me.

Many of my Christian friends urged me to take him back. They encouraged us to get more counseling. I so desperately wanted this second marriage to work that I was willing to do anything. I started seeing John again and decided to go to Owen Sound on weekends to spend time with him and his boys and give our sons a chance to see each other.

CONFRONTATION IN WIARTON

One Friday evening, as I was travelling from Cambridge to Owen Sound, I felt the Lord tell me to drive to Wiarton where the house was that he had bought with his girlfriend. I could not understand why the Lord would tell me that, because John had told me that he was going to rent that house out and that Kathy had moved out. I decided to listen to the Lord. I had learned after making many mistakes, that it is best to listen to that still small voice when He speaks.

I did not know where the house was located, but the Lord directed me very specifically how I should go and He led me right to the house on the north hill in Wiarton. I found John with Kathy working out in the garden and my two stepsons were there with them.

I confronted John in front of Kathy and told her that he had declared that she was a witch and that he did not love her and that he wanted nothing more to do with her. I asked him why he kept lying to me about their relationship. He got very angry and slapped me hard across the face in front of her and Michael and James. I started to cry and I said to him, "Why do you keep begging me to come back if you want her? Just leave me alone and stop lying to me!"

47

With that I turned to walk away. He kicked me so hard in the backside that I fell on the ground. I got up and started to walk quickly away towards my van parked several yards up the hill. Then I heard Michael and James yelling at me to run. Looking back, I was shocked to see John running after me. I ran as hard as I could. I desperately wanted to get Chad, Jeff and I safely away from him. By the time I made it to the van, my heart was pounding so hard I could hardly breathe, and I ended up having an asthma attack.

I drove to my mother's house, packed our things and drove back to Cambridge that night.

SECOND INCIDENT IN WIARTON

It was not long before he once again was asking me to forgive him and telling me that his relationship with Kathy was over. Again I believed him and started going to Owen Sound to visit him and the boys.

On another weekend, he told me that he had to go out to a horse fair on the Saturday evening. I was staying with my mother at the time and he was living with his father as we had rented out our farmhouse. As I was putting Jeffrey to bed, I heard the Lord tell me to drive to Wiarton to the house.

It was 10 p.m. I was scared half to death, but I decided to listen to my Heavenly Father. When I got to the house, I did not see John's truck. Kathy's car was parked in the driveway. All the lights were out in the house. I heard the Lord tell me to park my car way up the hill and walk back to the house. I felt like a burglar as I made my way to the living room window. By the light of the TV, I saw John and Kathy making out on the floor.

I saw red! I pounded on the front door. No one answered. I walked around to the back and started banging on the back door and yelling at them to let me in. I banged the door so hard that eventually I was able to break into the house. There they were —

Kathy with nothing more than a T-shirt on and John in a pair of shorts. Kathy threatened to call the police and at one point tried to dial, but John stopped her.

For the next hour, I went through one of the most painful discoveries I had ever been through. Kathy revealed to me the numerous times that John had lied and deceived me the entire year and a half that they had gone out before I found out about them. She told me about the car he had bought for her, about the weekend trips that he had taken her on, when he was supposed to be fishing with some of his friends. She told me about him phoning her on the Marriage Enrichment weekend, when he was supposed to be writing letters to me (he had tearfully renewed his marriage vows with me!). She shared with me how he had called her several times when we were in Florida and how much he loved her. She told me that they had slept at his mother's the night before and that he had begged her three times while they were making love to marry him.

When she was finished telling me all these hurtful things, I felt like I just wanted to die. I said to John, "Why do you keep begging me to come back? Why do you keep telling me how much you love me and that you want nothing more to do with her? Please, leave me alone. Please do not call me any more. Please let me go so that I can heal and go on with my life; I can't take the pain any longer."

He said he did not know what he wanted. He said that he loved us both. I told him that he could not have us both and I walked out.

I look back on that incident now and wonder how Kathy could have really known at a heart level what she and John were doing to the life of a family. Did they ever stop to think about what the effects would on our four little boys? I believe the devastation of the breakup of a family can be one of the most hurtful things a person can endure in their lifetime. I know that my children years later still suffer from it. Our extended families were also very much hurt by the breakdown of our marriage. Where do people go who do not have Jesus?

ANOTHER TRY WITH JOHN

Over the next two weeks he called several times pleading with me to take him back and telling me the relationship with Kathy was over again. He would tell me how much the boys were missing us. I told him that I did not feel that I could ever trust him again.

One night, approximately two weeks after I had found John and Kathy together, I received another phone call from him. This time we spoke only for a second and then he said he had to go because someone was at the door and he hung up.

The next thing I knew, he was at my front door weeping and clutching his Bible to his chest. He had the Bible open at Proverbs 5, and he started quoting scripture about what happens to a person when they get involved in adulterous relationships. He begged me on his knees to take him back. He said that we could get counseling from a Christian counselor of my choosing and that he would do whatever the counselor suggested to make things work.

We were given the name of an excellent man in Kitchener and decided to go and see him. On our first visit John waited in the waiting room and was asked to read the book, Why Christians Commit Adultery, by John and Paula Sandford. In the meantime, I told the counselor exactly what had been going on and the details of the affair.

Eventually, the counselor called John into the room and bluntly said to my husband, "Mister, I don't know what your wife is still doing with you. You are a liar and a cheat, and unless you are willing to be accountable for all your actions and comply with a list of things that you and Lynn will agree to, then I will work night and day, seven days a week to help her get away from you.

What you have put her through is emotional abuse and we will not stand for it any longer!" I was so shocked by his strong rebuke of John and, quite frankly, so was John.

However, John agreed to the list of things that we felt were fair, which included having absolutely nothing to do with Kathy, either by phone, meeting her or any other form of correspondence. He was to be accountable to me regarding his whereabouts and I was to have complete freedom in questioning what he was doing without him getting angry and telling me that I did not trust him.

The first month went fairly well. It was August, and we had some nice times with the boys. He visited us in Cambridge and we spent time in Owen Sound.

In September, I noticed his attitude started changing towards me again. He was not as interested in getting together as much and would get angry if I questioned him. I discovered that he had been in contact with Kathy, but he said it had to do with the house and some furniture they had bought together. In early September, we both agreed that perhaps we needed some time apart. For the next two months, life was a blur. I would go to work, try to function as well as possible. Chad and Jeff would cry themselves to sleep every night. I would go from one to the other trying to console them because they missed their Dad and brothers so much. Then I would go to bed and weep until I fell asleep.

The man who was my direct boss at work was a fine Christian person who had walked with the Lord for over 30 years. He was the Director of Operations for our company and we often drove together to the nursing home facilities that we were in charge of. How I praise God for this man's encouragement, guidance and mercy that he extended to me during that most difficult time of my life! He cried with me, he gave me fatherly advice, and never once judged or criticized me. He was a fine example of a happily married man who loved God, and his family and knew what priorities were important.

JOHN'S AFFAIR WITH MARY

In November of 1990, my husband once again started calling and telling me that he still loved me and wanted me back. Our sixth anniversary was coming up November 23rd, and he asked me if he could take me out on a date. He came down to Cambridge, took me to the classiest restaurant in the area, bought me roses and talked me into moving back to Owen Sound. I was so lonely and feeling like such a failure that I was again listening to him.

After dinner we went back to my house and made love. Afterwards, when John was having a bath, the phone rang. A young girl's voice said, "This is Mary Smith." I was very surprised to hear from her. I had taught her Pioneer Girls years before in our church and I wondered what she would be doing calling me. (She was now approximately 19 years old). She explained that she had been dating my husband the last two months and that he had asked her to marry him. She was just wondering when our divorce was coming through so that she could make plans. Well I was so upset that I saw red. I went into the bathroom and told John, in no uncertain terms to get the "you know what" out of my house. I was so angry I smashed the towel rack off of the wall with my fist.

After arguing with me for about half an hour, he left. I collapsed in a puddle of tears. I do not know what it was that I said to my mother later on that night, but she ended up coming down and staying with me for a couple of days because she was so worried about my state of mind. I just felt like I did not want to go on living any more.

I went into work the next day and ended up breaking down in front of some of my co-workers. They were quite concerned for me and one of the women offered to lend me a book that she said would help me. She brought it into work the next day and I took it home to read.

THE NEW AGE BOOK

Almost from the first page, I found that the book gave me the creeps. I read a couple of chapters and discovered that this book was New Age. It said things like, if you pinned a piece of cloth on the inside of your shirt everyday for three months, things would change and get better for you. If you wrote the day the three months would be up in your calendar and then believe that things were going to turn around for you, they would. Man, it was a weird book! After reading it a short while, I put it beside myself on the bed deciding to return it to the woman in the morning and went to sleep.

When I woke up the first thing I noticed is that the little blue book was gone. I thought it had slipped off of the bed and so I got up to look for it because I wanted to return it to the woman at work. I looked everywhere in that room and could not find it. I tore the bedclothes off, searched under the bed and looked in the other rooms of the house and it was nowhere to be found. Off and on throughout the next couple of weeks, I looked for the book but to no avail.

CHAPTER 10

"THAT MAN IS GOING TO BE SIGNIFICANT IN YOUR LIFE"

I will repay you for the years the locusts have eaten "
Joel 2:25

My girlfriend, Sharon Coburn, had been telling me for months that she thought I should go to a Church in Cambridge called "The Vineyard". I thought it sounded like a wine store or something, but she explained that it was a wonderful, contemporary church that would be able to help me. I said that I was not really in a place to meet new people, but she told me that they had a great ministry to the poor and that I would probably enjoy helping others.

It was getting closer to Christmas and I knew that I had a bad attitude and needed to get right with God. I called a mutual friend of ours that was now living in Cambridge and attending The Vineyard and she said that she would be happy to take me on Sunday.

My introduction to the Cambridge Vineyard was like nothing I had ever experienced before. All of my life, I had attended formal churches where they sang from hymnals and where the whole service was completely structured. The first thing I noticed was everyone was dressed very casually; blue jeans were the norm. Everyone was chatting and they were very friendly and welcoming. Everyone seemed to be drinking coffee. They met in a school auditorium, and there was a band on stage. I had never seen anything like it.

The music team leader welcomed us and asked us to stand. Then the most beautiful heavenly worship started to play. I began to weep. All through the worship, I could feel the Spirit of God on me in a wonderful way. I wept and cried out to God and repented to Him for not listening to Him and not walking in His ways the past few years. I felt an incredible peace come over me and I knew that I had finally come to the right place.

After the worship, the pastor got up and gave one of the most casual, non-threatening sermons that I had ever heard. It was refreshing and really made me think about my relationship to God as a Father, something that I had not really thought much about.

When the service was over, people came over to me and hugged me and asked me if they could pray for me. It was so wonderful to feel accepted and loved even in the terrible depressed state that I was in.

I was standing at the back of the auditorium just looking around when I saw this tall, dark, handsome man walking around talking to people. I heard, what I believed to be the audible voice of God, say to me, "That man is going to be significant in your life."

The first thing I thought was, "What does that mean?" I no more wanted to meet another good looking man than fly to the moon, thank you very much!

"THAT MAN IS GOING TO BE SIGNIFICANT IN YOUR LIFE"

I went home that Sunday feeling as if I had hope for the first time in months.

BAPTISMAL SERVICE

That afternoon my husband brought our son Jeffrey back from Owen Sound. He asked me if he could talk to me and I agreed. He asked me if I would pray with him and if I would forgive him for what he had done to me.

I said, "Yes, John, I choose to forgive you because God tells me that I am to forgive, but forgiving does not mean taking you back. I don't believe that God wants me to keep subjecting myself to such emotional abuse. I can't stand it any longer."

Just before he was ready to leave, he asked me what I was doing that night. I told him about the Vineyard and that they were having a baptism service that night and I was going to it. He asked me if he could go. I said it was open to everyone, so he could come.

It was a wonderful time until right near the end of the baptisms. All of a sudden, John got up out of his seat climbed over the first two rows of chairs and went up into the baptismal tank and asked the pastor if he would baptize him. I was so shocked that I did not know what to do.

John started to share in front of everyone what a horrible sinner he had been but that he was not going to do it any more. I started to cry. The poor pastor looked as if he did not know what to do, but proceeded to baptize him. I was so upset because now I thought that all these new people would make me feel that I had to take him back again. Man was I ever confused! During the next week I had no peace at all from God.

FIRST CONTACT WITH PASTOR BOLTON

That week I allowed John to come down and attend a midweek meeting with me. While John and I were sitting in the meeting, a couple came over to us and asked us if we would like to go over to their house for coffee. After arriving there and starting to share with them about our circumstances, the lady said to us that there was a man living in their basement who used to be the Pastor of the Cambridge Vineyard by the name of Dale Bolton. As soon as she said his name, the Lord showed me a picture of the tall, dark man that he had spoken to me about on Sunday. She shared with us how Dale's wife had left him and their children two and a half years before and had an affair with one of Dale's friends. Carol felt that perhaps Dale might be able to counsel us and we agreed to meet him the following Sunday at church.

John came down the following Sunday to meet this Pastor Bolton. When Carol walked up to us with Dale, I knew who he was going to be before we were even introduced. It was the man that the Lord had told me about who would be significant in my life. Carol introduced us and Dale spoke mainly to John. He said that he would be happy to meet with us sometime. That night John went back up to Owen Sound.

CHAPTER 11

"ASK THE LORD FOR A SIGN"

*Gideon replied, "If now I have found favor in your eyes,
give me a sign that it is really you talking to me.*
Judg 6:17

The following night, as I was telling a girlfriend on the phone that I was having absolutely no peace from God about seeing my husband, she said to me, "Why don't you ask God for a sign?"

"What do you mean 'a sign'?"

Lee replied, "Ask God for confirmation as to whether or not you are supposed to take your husband back."

I thought that was a wise idea. When I got off the phone, I prayed to God and told him that I needed a sign from him but I did not even know what to ask for. God spoke audibly to me and told me to ask him to find the book I had lost three weeks ago. I almost laughed because God is so practical and so amazing at the same time. So I said, "Okay God, now let me get this straight, if You find that book for me, it means that I am not to take John back,"

He said, "Yes". Within a couple of seconds I heard Him speaking to me again. "Get out of bed and look under the bed on the right side on the floor".

"Lord, it's not there. I've looked there ten times!"

He kept prompting me to get out bed and look on the floor under the right-hand side of the bed, but I kept arguing with him.

After a few minutes, I decided I had better listen to Him. I got out of bed. I went to the bottom of the bed, bent down, and saw that little blue book lying on the floor under the right hand side of the bed. I was so shocked and when I picked that book up both my hands were shaking. I could not believe how amazing God was and how faithful He had been to me.

I also had a hard time understanding that the God of all forgiveness was telling me to end my marriage. It was quite close to Christmas and I had promised our boys that we could spend Christmas together. We went up to Owen Sound a few days before Christmas. I kept praying that God would continue to reveal His truth to me and told God that as soon as Christmas was over, I would definitely end the relationship with John.

CHRISTMAS DISCOVERY

On the day before Christmas, I went shopping at one of the malls in Owen Sound to get something from John for my two boys. To my surprise, I ran into the nineteen-year old girl that I had taught in Pioneer Girls and who had started the second affair with John. She walked up to me and asked me if John had told me about their romp in the sack the previous Monday night (the night the Lord gave me the Sign about the book).

Furious, I drove back to where John and the boys were and confronted him with this latest allegation.

He denied it. We drove up to the mall to talk to Mary. They stood outside the Grey County Mall in a snowstorm, arguing whether or not what she had said was true. John finally admitted she was telling the truth and on Christmas Eve, 1990, he drove Chad, Jeff, and me back to Cambridge.

That night when I went to bed, I felt the most amazing peace. I prayed and asked God to help my boys not to be upset tomorrow morning when they woke up, and he answered my prayer.

The next day was a beautiful peaceful day, although I did cry a couple of times when the boys were not around. I cried over the death of a dream. I cried for the boys, both his and mine who were so innocent and yet so wounded by our mistakes. I cried for our extended families that were so shaken up and hurt by the breakdown of our family and I cried because I felt that I had once again let God down. I also wept tears of relief knowing that, finally, I was walking in His will. I wept out of a thankful heart for all that He had done for me. I had this wonderful anticipation in the pit of my stomach that God was allowing me to turn a corner of my life that would enable me to become closer to Him than I had ever known before. I actually started believing that the best was yet to be.

Little did I know what He had in store for me.

PART III

BEAUTY
FOR ASHES

CHAPTER 12

COURTSHIP WITH "THAT SIGNIFICANT MAN"

*He has sent me to bind up the brokenhearted, to proclaim
freedom for the captives and release from darkness for the
prisoners, to proclaim the year of the Lord's favor and the day
of vengeance of our God, to comfort all who mourn, and
provide for those who grieve in Zion— to bestow on them a
crown of beauty instead of ashes, the oil of gladness instead
of mourning, and a garment of praise instead of a spirit of
despair. They will be called oaks of righteousness, a planting
of the LORD for the display of his splendor.*
Isa 61:1b,-3

Over the next couple of months, God started a work in me
that was truly incredible. He brought that significant
man, Dale Bolton, into my life to help me to understand
what it was to walk through the kind of pain and brokenness that
only one who has experienced unfaithfulness can understand.
Dale helped me to see that God understood my pain because he
had experienced the unfaithfulness of Israel. He helped me to

understand what it really meant to know Christ and to totally surrender my will and my strength to Him.

As Dale and I got to know each other, it was not very long before we both realized that God had brought us together for a specific purpose. Our courtship started as a special friendship and we grew closer to each other as we sought God on the issues that I was going through in my life.

When I first met Dale, I found out from some people in our church that he was probably one of the most sought after eligible bachelors in the Cambridge Vineyard. He had been seeing a few of the women for coffee but had made it very clear to them that he only wanted to be friends. (That is what he believed they understood).

After a time, he realized that he was just getting into more hot water than he cared to think about with this approach, and so he asked God to show him the kind of girl that would find it easy to live with him. The Lord gave him five specific things that were important for Dale; he decided to make an acronym out of them. They just happened to spell "LADIE":

L — leadership.

A — attractive (as if he needed that for the girl to find it easy to live with him!).

D — doer — the woman would enjoy doing some of the fun, crazy things that he liked to do.

I — for innovative.

E — endurance — he wanted to make sure that next women he married would be there for the long haul.

After the Lord had showed him these five things, he realized that none of the ladies he was having coffee with fit the bill; so he decided to change his process and stop having coffee just for friendship. (The funny thing is Dale does not even drink coffee!). Shortly after this, Dale and I met and he discovered fairly quickly that I fit all of the things on this list.

Of course, I did not know that I was being analyzed at this time. Nor did I realize that over the next several weeks, Dale was asking God to show him all the things that he liked or respected about me and that we had in common. Dale later told me he stopped journaling the things the Lord showed him when he reached 140!

"I WILL CHANGE YOUR NAME"

I believe the first time that Dale and I really understood that God had brought us together was on New Year's Eve, 1990. Our friends were holding a wedding in their home for a good friend of Dale's. Dale was the best man and Carol had asked me to come to the wedding because I did not have anything to do that evening.

It was one of the most beautiful weddings I had ever been to. When Garland and Kari were saying their vows, they asked everyone in the room to sing, "I will change your name" to each other.

While all the couples in the room were singing to each other, I started to cry. I was in such a bad place emotionally that my heart felt like it was breaking. I looked up with tears streaming down my cheeks. My eyes met Dale's from across the room. It was like time stood still. I felt the Lord tell me that everything would be okay, that He would change my name from outcast and wounded, lonely and afraid to confident, joyfulness, overcoming one, faithfulness, friend of God, one who seeks His face. (The words to the song, "I Will Change Your Name")

"DO YOU WANT TO DANCE?"

Over the next few weeks Dale and I spent a fair amount of time together. One night while visiting friends, everyone decided to dance on the cement floor of their basement. We put on some lovely old dance tunes and danced and waltzed for hours.

Dale and I danced great together and we had so much fun. My, it was good to laugh after all the years of hurt. It was great to be able to dance, knowing that God was smiling down on us instead of frowning. I was being so set free from the religion that I had carried around with me for years. By the end of the evening, we had danced so much on that cement floor that I had worn large holes in the bottom of both my socks. We laughed and laughed. Talk about dancing your socks off!

The next day when I got home from work, I found a package with three new pairs of socks in it, with a note that read, "Do you want to dance?" We were just like a couple of teenagers.

I learned that this new man in my life was a wild maniac when it came to participatory sports like kayaking, camping, scuba diving, and downhill skiing. When he told me that he wanted to parachute someday, I said that I would start with downhill skiing! Many times we talked for hours on end about God, our past, and our future together.

THE PARK CHAT

Approximately one month after we started dating, Dale asked me to write out on paper what love meant to me and he would do the same. Dale picked me up at work for a lunch picnic in his car that he called "the Black Stallion" and we shared our letters that we had written about the meaning of love.

It was then that he told me that he felt he needed to put our relationship on hold. He was concerned that I might become an idol to him, and he did not want to put anything before God in his life.

I started to cry when he told me. I had been expecting him to reject me since I had met him and I had grown to care for him so much. He was crying too. When he left me at the door of my office building, I told him that I understood why he was doing this. Then for the first time I told him that I loved him and he then told me he loved me too.

I went back to work that afternoon with mixed feelings. I felt great that he had finally told me that he loved me, and yet I was confused regarding what our future would hold.

That weekend my children were visiting their father, and so I had a lot of time alone with God. On Saturday, I decided to go swimming; as I was sitting in the crowded hot tub at the community pool, I heard God's audible voice again. He said to me, "I am preparing you for Dale in the same way that I am preparing the Bride for My Son." The most incredible peace came upon me and I knew that someday we would be together.

Within a couple of days, Dale had sought God about our relationship and came to the understanding that it was okay for us to continue to see each other. Boy was I glad that we did not have to wait too long because we were fast becoming best friends.

"IF NOT FOR THE GRACE OF GOD THERE GO I"

After Dale and I had been dating a short while, I knew that I was going to have to tell him about the abortion. I felt sick to my stomach every time I thought about telling him because I felt that he would think I was the most horrible person in the world and reject me for sure.

As I prayed about it one day, God told me that everything would be all right if I told Dale. That night when he came over to visit, I sat down with him and shared the story about what had happened with the abortion. He listened so carefully. When I was finished, he just held me in his arms and let me cry. He conveyed to me how sorry he was that I had gone through such a difficult thing.

The next day when I got home from work, there was a beautiful letter waiting for me. In the letter, he told me that he did not judge me in any way. He knew that, if not for the grace of God, he might have done the same thing.   He was so loving and kind. God used Dale's reaction to the abortion to continue to bring healing into my life.

CHAPTER 13

"I WANT TO BE
HEALED LORD"

If the Son therefore shall make you free,
you shall be free indeed.
John 8:36

I had never heard of Inner Healing and Deliverance prior to going to the Vineyard. Suddenly, I was on a radical learning curve. I desperately wanted to be healed of my past. I wanted to let go of the pain and learn to be what God wanted me to be. No longer did I want to be a victim. I sought my healing with a vengeance and God was faithful to heal me.

One of the first things I did was attend a small conference put on by the Stratfford Vineyard called, "The Father Heart of God". I had always known the love of Jesus ever since I was a Christian, but I had really struggled with the love of God the Father because I often related him to my own father and thought that he was unapproachable.

During that conference, I came to understand that I was responsible for my reactions to my father, and I had to ask God to forgive me for judging and dishonouring my Dad and for holding unforgiveness in my heart towards him. I also had to choose to forgive him for being critical of me and for not being the affectionate loving Dad that I thought he should have been.

The Lord gave me a revelation that the reason my Dad was not affectionate with us children was because it was his way of protecting himself from being hurt again. He had lost several brothers and sisters as a boy growing up and he just could not handle getting too close for fear of being emotionally wounded again. God helped me to love my Dad in a fresh, new way and He helped me to become closer to him than I would have even imagined.

When one of the sessions was over, people who wanted prayer were asked to move out into the aisles. As soon as I did, I felt the spirit of God so strongly on me that I fell to my knees. No one came to pray for me that day, but God ministered to me so powerfully that I began speaking in tongues for the very first time. I was so thrilled because I had been asking God for about a month for this gift but had not yet ever spoken in tongues. It was great to be set free from so much bondage and fear.

It was shortly after this time that I heard the Lord tell me one day in my car to write my Dad a letter. In that letter, I was to tell my Dad how much God loved him and that God wanted him to accept His Son Jesus as his Saviour. God also told me to tell him that I understood why he had not been able to show love and affection. A few days after writing the letter, I had a message on my answering machine from my Dad thanking me for the letter and telling me that he loved me. I think it was the first time my Dad told me he loved me without my initiating it. It made me weep.

The Counseling Schools that I attended at Singing Waters over the next few months were life changing for me. Fletch and Betty Fletcher were a wonderful couple, who had also been through divorce several times and knew what it was like to experience the pain that I was going through. I felt comfortable with them and knew at a heart level that they understood the place that I was in. They taught from the teachings of John and Paula Sandford of the United States.

The revelation that God brought was unbelievable. I was amazed at how everything that they were teaching could be applied to my life. I felt as if my whole life story could be told using the four scriptural laws that they were teaching — things like honouring your parents, judging others, and the law of sowing and reaping. I learned about how our lives can be drastically affected by making inner vows and by having bitter root judgments and expectations.

The best part was that I learned that I could get off the roller coaster of bad choices and stop reaping the consequences from the judgments and negative sowing that I had done.

I also learned how Jesus had delivered people from demons. I came to understand that demons could affect us and have a right to stay and harass us when we walk in unrepented sin or when we go through traumatic experiences. During one of the sessions, I realized that I had of spirit of "expecting to be rejected" from experiencing so much rejection in my life. I had believed the lie that this demonic presence was telling me that all men would reject me and that I was not worthy to be loved. I expected Dale to reject me. Every time he would tell me he loved me, I would tell him I loved him, too; but deep inside, I would be thinking, "Yah sure, one of these days he's going to tell me it's all over — just like the others." He could sense this spirit of rejection in me. God allowed him to see it and to fight against it so that he would not turn against me.

That same day, Fletch came over to me and said that God was delivering me from a spirit of rejection. He told that thing to get out of me. As it came out of the innermost depths of my being, I wailed and screamed, and it felt like my insides were going to come out of me. Fletch said that God was pulling an arrow out of my heart; and that, when He was finished, there would not even be a scar left. I felt this intense pain in my chest and I screamed as I literally felt something being pulled from my heart.

When it was over I was emotionally exhausted and as limp as a dishrag. I slept long and deeply that night. When I got up the next morning, the first thing that I noticed was that I no longer had the heavy pain in my chest that I had carried the past couple of years. The wounding that I had experienced when I found out my husband was having an affair was like a knife in my heart, and I had been walking around with emotional pain that was as real and as painful as physical pain. It was so wonderful to be set free.

During this time I was being awakened to the love of God the Father, in a new and powerful way. I came to understand His forgiveness and the amazing gift of his grace.

CHAPTER 14

WILL YOU MARRY ME?

My lover spoke and said to me, "Arise, my darling,
my beautiful one, and come with me. See! The winter
is past; the rains are over and gone. Flowers appear
on the earth; the season of singing has come, the cooing
of doves is heard in our land. The fig tree forms its
early fruit; the blossoming vines spread their fragrance.
Arise, come, my darling; my beautiful one, come with me."
My lover spoke and said to me, "Arise, my darling,
my beautiful one, and come with me.
Song 2:10-13

The day that I was delivered from a spirit of rejection, Dale and I went out for a walk in the beautiful woods surrounding Singing Waters. We were walking along the river on the property and it was there that this wonderful man of God asked me to marry him. I was so happy. I could not believe that he would want me for his wife. We were both so thankful to God for giving us to each other. We truly believed that God had given us a special gift in each other.

During this time I went to just about every conference I could attend that dealt with healing and walking out of brokenness. I attended a Christian twelve-step program in Kitchener that was being taught by Art Zelstra.

DIVORCE FROM JOHN

One night, when I was driving home in my car from a counseling session, I heard God's voice tell me the steps that I was to take to get my divorce from John. John had been fighting me regarding the divorce and had stated that he would not give me one. We were worth several hundred thousand dollars in assets and property, and he was not willing to part with any of it. God told me to ask him for a quick divorce based on adultery. He said that, if John would sign that he had committed adultery, then I was to ask for only $150,000 and not request any ongoing child support. I was to ask for one dollar per year alimony for myself and he would be able to have Jeffrey every second weekend, four weeks in the summer, and one-week at Christmas and the March break.

I said to God, "Father, You've got to be kidding, he'll never go for that and I should really get a lot more than that, financially."

But the Lord replied, "Go home and phone John and tell him what I have just told you, and he will agree with it."

So I went home, called John, told him what God had said and, with very little conflict, he agreed to the things that God had told me. Within three months time, I had my divorce and, in June of 1991, I received my divorce papers.

I cried that day. I wept for the death of a dream, I cried for our children and the ongoing pain that they were going through, and I cried for the lost years of my life that I had wasted out of God's will. I purposed at that time to ask God to help me to hear His voice and seek his face in every situation in my life so that I would never again walk in my own willful ways or walk away from Him again. And I cried for joy at being free to marry Dale.

PART IV

A NEW
BEGINNING

CHAPTER 15

THE YEAR OF
THE LORD'S FAVOUR

. . . he has sent me to bring good news to the oppressed,
to bind up the brokenhearted, to proclaim liberty to the c
aptives, and release to the prisoners; to proclaim
the year of the Lord's favor, . . .
Isaiah 61:1,2

O nce my divorce was through, we started making plans
for a wedding. Initially, Dale had teased me that we
should wait at least two years to get married. After all,
that is what all the divorce recovery manuals said to do. So I
agreed, but it seemed that the date we chose just started to get
closer and closer. We picked a date in December, but could not
get the hall and church at the same time. We chose a date in
November, but that fell through as well.

Finally, the only date that was suitable was on Friday,
October 11, 1991. At first, I was totally blown away by the
thought of having our wedding on the same day that I had had the
abortion. But God showed me that this was a special gift from

Him. He showed me that He was taking the horrible memory of that date and turning it into a glorious testimony of His loving kindness. He was taking the ashes of my life and making them into something beautiful. He showed me that what the devil had intended for bad in my life, He could make into something good. I truly came to understand the reality of the merciful, loving, heart of my Heavenly Father. I saw His mercy and forgiveness extended to me in such a way that I could not even comprehend it at that time.

Our wedding was mostly planned by my romantic honey Dale. I think he had been conjuring up in his mind for some time what he thought his next wedding would look like.

He suggested one day as we were driving in the car that he should sing to me as I walked down the aisle. I laughed out loud because I couldn't believe he would have the nerve. Then he suggested that we sing to each other during our vows. Man, I was really shocked!

Anyway, it happened just as he had dreamed. On October 11, 1991, I ran down the aisle into my lover's arms in front of two hundred and fifty of our beloved friends and family. Many people said it was the most romantic wedding they had ever been to. John Arnott officiated at our ceremony and Carol his wife was my matron of honour. Our four children were all part of our wedding party. Even Jeffrey looked smashing in his little tuxedo.

We drove two hours in a snowstorm to spend our first night at a lovely hotel in Richmond Hill. The next evening, we attended *Les Miserables* at the Royal Alexander Theatre. The following day, we set out on a 7-day Caribbean cruise. What a wonderful, romantic way it was to begin our life together!

It was not until a few years later, when God asked me to start telling people about the abortion, that I really understood the significance of the date of our wedding. The Lord told me to turn to Deuteronomy 15, verses 1 and 2:

THE YEAR OF THE LORD'S FAVOUR

At the end of every seven years you must cancel debts.
This is how it is to be done: Every creditor shall cancel
the loan he has made to his fellow Israelite. He shall not
require payment from his fellow Israelite or brother,
because the Lord's time for canceling debts has been pro-
claimed.

God showed me that not only had I been forgiven for the
abortion but that the debt had been cancelled. I wept with a
thankful heart to My Lord who had given so much so that I might
be redeemed. In Isaiah 61: the Lord showed me that October 11,
1991 was the Year of the Lord's Favour in my life. He told me
that He would use the testimony of what He had done to bind up
the broken hearted, to release the prisoners from captivity and to
bring hope to the hopeless.

He first asked me to share about the abortion at a daylong
workshop at Singing Waters. I thought that was special, as I had
received so much healing in that place. The first time I spoke out
loud to that group about the fact that I had had an abortion, I
thought I was going to vomit. But God gave me His grace and
strength. He told me that, if I was willing to share my testimony
of what He had done in my life, then He would bring healing not
only to me but healing to the nations.

As I have shared this testimony of his mercy and great grace
in my life, I have watched Him do miraculous things in the lives
of other people. He has brought hope to people who believed that
their sin was too great to ever be forgiven. He has brought the
prodigals home by showing them, through my story, His faithfulness and never-ending love.

HIS FROM THE TIME YOU WERE LITTLE

My first year at Vineyard family camp proved to be a very
exciting and wonderful time for me. It was there that I discovered

during a deliverance session with Graham Powell that I had actually become a Christian as a little girl.

Graham and I had stopped to take a rest half way through the ministry session. He was sitting, looking at me and all of a sudden, he got big tears in his eyes. He told me that God had just told him that I had been His (God's) since I was a little girl. Graham said to go back to my room and ask the Lord to show me how it had happened.

The Lord showed me a picture of myself at the age of six, standing with my hands folded. I had two pigtails in my hair and I looked very serious. It was at Dixon Hall and I was singing the song "Come Into My Heart, Lord Jesus". I knew then that was when Jesus became my Saviour. But it was not until the age of 27 that He actually became the Lord of my life.

FIRSTFRUITS — THE JOY OF THE LORD IS MY STRENGTH

Vineyard summer camps always proved to be great times of revelation for me. My second year at camp, 1993, Dale and I had been married a little over a year. There were wonderful meetings and speakers every morning and evening. I was learning so much and growing so close to my Heavenly Father.

One night, a speaker from Nicaragua was teaching and he had a call for people to go forward for prayer. I went up as usual because I was so hungry for more of God and Ray prayed for me. All of a sudden, I started to laugh and could not stop. I had never experienced anything like it before and did not quite know what to make of it. All I knew was that I had never felt so happy and joyful in my whole life and I knew that it was God who was causing me to laugh this way.

At one point someone came up to me and told me that Dale was back in our lodge room sick with the flu, but all I could do is laugh. Being a nurse, this was totally out of character for me, but somehow I knew that God was in control and that he would look after my husband for me. John Arnott was not sure at the time what on earth was going on in me. As he watched, I began praying for other people. Fairly soon, everyone else had the Holy Laughter. It was an amazing time.

John Arnott now says that I was the first fruit of the renewal that has been spreading all over the world since 1994. I believe that the laughter that year was the miraculous healing power of God, moving in me and bringing me to a deeper level of understanding His love and acceptance of me.

CHAPTER 16

"I'LL NEVER MOVE BACK TO TORONTO!"

*Trust in the LORD with all your heart and lean not on
your own understanding; in all your ways acknowledge
him, and he will make your paths straight.*
Prov 3:5-6

During the first year of our marriage, God started speaking to Dale about planting a new church in Toronto. When I had moved away from Toronto at the age of twenty-one, I had said that I would never move back to Toronto. Now it seemed that God was calling us to the one place that I did not want to go. But I prayed about it and asked God to open up a job in Toronto if that was where He wanted us to be.

Dale started driving to the North of Toronto to pray through the streets on a weekly basis. Dale asked God, if He wanted us to come to the Thornhill/Richmond Hill area, to send us someone who would invite us or be interested in us coming to the area to start a Vineyard.

One day we received a phone call from a Mr. Dennis Jones. He told Dale that he had been at a Vineyard meeting in Barrie on the weekend and had run into a man named Bob Nickling. Dennis had asked Bob if he knew of anyone who would be interested in starting a Vineyard in the Thornhill area. Bob said, "There just so happens to be a pastor who is praying through the streets of Thornhill on a regular basis to see if it is where God wants to plant a Vineyard Church."
Bob gave Dennis our phone number and he contacted us.

Within a few days, we met Dennis and Elizabeth Jones, a lovely English couple, who attended Emmanuel Anglican church in Richvale. They had been praying that God would send someone to plant a Vineyard in their area. Dale agreed to get together with them and others who were interested to intercede for the start up of this new church plant, and the Thornhill Vineyard was conceived.

THE JOB FROM HEAVEN
Around that same time, I saw an advertisement in the Globe and Mail for the position of Administrator at a large seniors' complex in Scarborough. I was working at Versa Care's head office in Cambridge as a Nursing Consultant and had always dreamt of using my administrator's skills obtained taking an administrator's course several years previous. I applied for the position and when I got down to the final interview stage, I discovered that 350 other people had applied for the job.

I knew for sure after they had awarded me the position that God's hand was in it. There were several other people who were more qualified in education and experience than I was, who had also been shortlisted for the job.

My position at The Wexford turned out to be "the job from heaven". The Board of Directors was lovely to work with, the staff were non-unionized and very easy to get along with, and the seniors were healthy people who enjoyed life to the fullest. I had always worked with the debilitated elderly, many of whom had Alzheimer's disease; so it was a real pleasure to be working with the well elderly.

Not long after I started my new job the Lord provided Dale and I a lovely home two doors down from where the Jones lived in Thornhill. God sure was answering prayer and opening doors for our move to Thornhill!

"I WANT YOU TO QUIT WORKING!"

Just before we moved to Thornhill, I heard God tell me one night in my bathtub in Cambridge that I was to quit working when that house in Cambridge sold. I was a little confused; we had just taken the house off the market because it had not sold in almost a year. We had been able to rent it out to a couple so that we could move to Thornhill. I had just started my "job from heaven" and so I had a hard time understanding what God had just spoken to me.

I said to Him, "What does that mean, Lord?" but I got no answer at that time. Consequently, I thought it must mean sometime in the future; so I would not worry about it. I told God that I was willing to quit when He told me it was time. However, down deep there was a certain hidden unwillingness; my job was an idol to me. My career had always been my security and my identity.

Anyway, life went on and every now and then I would ask God, "Is it time to put the house back on the market?"

The answer came, "When it is time to sell the house, I will do it and you won't even have to lift a finger." I decided then that I would not worry about it any longer.

Vineyard summer camp was approaching and I remember wondering what God is going to do in me this year. Mary Audrey Raycroft was teaching a course called "Born Free", which talks about giving our rights over to God and allowing Him to be on the throne instead of our self.

As I was meditating on what she was saying, God showed me that I had not been willing for him to take my job. My job had been too important to me. Even though I said with my head that I would give up my job, I really had not meant it with my heart. I knew that I was finally willing to allow God to take my job from me. I went forward at a meeting and I laid my job on the altar. I gave it back to God and told him that I was willing to let go of it for good.

The day we got home from camp, there were several messages on our answering machine. One of them was from a Real Estate man who had listed our house before. He asked us if we would be willing to sell our house because he thought that he had a buyer. Within one week the house was sold and "we didn't even have to lift a finger".

On Sept 1, 1993, the house sold. On Sept 15, I handed in my resignation to the Board of directors of The Wexford. They were very upset with me since I had only worked there for one and a half years and they had spent a large sum of money procuring me for the position of Administrator. I gave them three months notice and told them that I would help them to find a replacement. It was one of the saddest days I can remember.

"O YE OF LITTLE FAITH!"

Over the next three months, I constantly went to God to ask Him if I had heard him right. This was such a major decision that I had made and I wanted to make sure that I was in His perfect will. I was not only leaving a wonderful job where I was extremely happy, but I was giving up almost $70,000 in salary and benefits. When I quit working, it was just after the government brought in new legislation stating that if you quit a job you could not collect unemployment insurance. So I knew that I was going to go from having a very good income to almost nothing overnight. I believed that God was faithful; He had proven that many times, but still I kept asking Him to show me whether or not I was doing what He wanted me to.

SIGN AT WOMEN AGLOW

One of the times I asked for confirmation was when I was driving in my car on the way to speak at a Women Aglow meeting. I was singing a Vineyard praise song, one that I just loved, and I said to God, "Father, if I really heard you right about quitting my job, please let us sing this song tonight at the meeting." I felt that this was a good sign, because I had never heard them sing this specific song at a Women's Aglow meeting before. That night, during the second group of songs, we sang the very song that I had asked the Lord for us to sing. I had more peace in my spirit.

PROPHECY

However, as the months continued on, I became more and more anxious about giving up my job. I was letting go of a career that I had worked very hard to achieve and it had been my source of security and identity for many years. God understood my struggles during this time and He constantly was there for me.

Two weeks before I was to finish working, Dale and I were driving to a meeting at the home of John and Carol Arnott. Larry Randolph, a prophetic man, and his wife were going to be there to minister to a group of leaders from the Airport Vineyard Christian Fellowship. At that time we were still working part time at the Airport Church, and so we were excited about going to this meeting. On the drive over I prayed out loud with Dale, that if I really had heard God right about quitting my job and that if I was really in His will, then Larry would have a word for me from The Lord.

When we arrived at the meeting, several of us ministered to

Larry and his wife first. When we were finished, John asked Larry if he had a word for anyone in the room. Larry said, "I only have a word for this couple on my left." He pointed to Dale and I. He started off by saying something about Dale being like Jonathan and my being his armour bearer. Then he stopped and looked directly into my eyes and said, "The Lord wants you to know that you are in His perfect will; in fact, you couldn't be more in His will if you tried."

With that I started to cry. Then I began to laugh and the whole group ministered to me. Dale still laughs about this time. He said it showed a lack of faith on my part, but I like to think of it as a little girl asking her Daddy for reassurance. God was so good to answer me and so patient, as I struggled with some of the new things that were happening in my life.

CHAPTER 17

"DESIRE PROPHECY MORE THAN ANY OTHER GIFT"

*Follow the way of love and eagerly desire
spiritual gifts, especially the gift of prophecy.*
1 Cor 14:1

During the three months that I was getting ready to quit my job, God was preparing me in other wonderful ways.

One night Dale and I were having supper with Marc Dupont and his wife Kim. "Marc." I said, "I often hear Gods voice for myself, I have even heard His audible voice on occasion, but I would really like to hear him for other people. I want to have the experience that Joel talked about in Joel 2:28 and 29:

*And afterward, I will pour out my Spirit on all people.
Your sons and daughters will prophesy, your old men will
dream dreams, your young men will see visions. Even on
my servants, both men and women, I will pour out my
Spirit in those days.*

Marc responded, "Lynn, prophecy is a gift like any other gift from the Holy Spirit. Do you believe your father in heaven wants to give you his good and perfect gifts?"

"Yes!"

"Then ask him for it."

From that day on, for three weeks straight, I prayed that God would give me a gift of prophecy. I asked him to give me dreams and visions and allow me to hear His voice to edify and build up others in the body of Christ.

MY FIRST PROPHECY

Shortly after, as I was driving along in my car, not really thinking about anything significant, I heard God speak to me about Jeremy Sinnot, the worship leader at The Airport Vineyard. He told me to tell Jeremy that God would be increasing His anointing on him in the area of worship and songwriting.

The next Sunday I shared with Jeremy what the Lord had told me and it blessed him so much. He said it was real confirmation to something that he had been crying out to the Lord for. Man, was I excited!

DREAMS

Over the next few days, I had a couple of very significant dreams. In one of the dreams I was in the auditorium of the old Airport Vineyard church building. The place was full of people who were worshipping and singing the song, "Show Your Power". The Spirit of God was hovering over the crowd but He was grieved, and I heard Him say to the people (although they could not hear Him):

"You ask me to show my power to you, but you are the

ones who are limiting My power by your fears and unbelief. Let go of your fears, let go of your agendas, let go
of your unbelief and see if I will pour out My Spirit upon
this land."

When I woke up, I journaled what the Lord had shown me.
As He instructed me, I shared the dream at The Airport Vineyard
church the following Sunday.

CHAPTER 18

THE OPEN VISION —
OCTOBER 16, 1993

As soon as you began to pray, an answer was given,
which I have come to tell you, for you are highly esteemed.
Therefore, consider the message and understand the vision:
Dan 9:23

On October 16, 1993, at 12:30 a.m., I was laying in bed wide awake, as my son Chad had just been up to the bathroom sick. I was praying for him, when all of a sudden I saw before my open eyes what appeared to be a huge technicolour screen (much like what you would see at the movies.) Initially, I did not know what was happening, but I later discovered that what I was experiencing was an open vision from the Lord.

In this vision, I saw before me a long canyon, which went as far as the eye could see into the distance. This canyon, or pit, was filled with dark, muddy liquid. All around the edge of this pit were hundreds of thousands of people. Some of them I recognized right away, for many were part of the church that I knew. Others I had never seen before but I knew in my spirit that they were part of the body of Christ. I was in the vision, and yet I was looking in on it as well.

On the right of this large canyon was a rocky precipice that went up and flattened out on to a rocky ledge or plateau. I could see the angels in the heavenly realms. There was a little cherub flitting back and forth talking to several angels that were gathering and looking down at the scene below.

All of a sudden, fully clothed people started coming out of the muddy liquid in this pit. They started calling out to us, "Help me! Save me!" Those of us on the edge started pulling them out of the muddy liquid. It seemed to be a somewhat easy process. They just kept on coming out, thousands upon thousands of them.

As they came out of the mud and mire, they started rejoicing and praising God saying, "Praise God, we are saved!" Then they climbed up and on to the rocky ledge on the right and were hugging each other.

As this was happening, the angels in the heavens were all excited and singing and praising God for what He was doing. The spirit of God was hovering over the whole scene. It was breathtakingly beautiful — almost too amazing to describe!

I decided to journal what I had just witnessed and asked God to show me what he was saying in this vision. He said, "What I have just shown you is a picture from Psalm 40. I turned to Psalm 40 and this is what I read:

> *(1) I waited patiently for the LORD; he turned to me and heard my cry.*
> *(2) He lifted me out of the slimy pit, out of the mud and mire; he set my feet on a rock and gave me a firm place to stand.*
> *(3) He put a new song in my mouth, a hymn of praise to our God. Many will see and fear and put their trust in the LORD.*

Then He continued on:

"Many of my chosen people are in the miry pit. They are covered with the mud and mire of their own sins, of Satan's strongholds, of the things of the world that they are holding onto so dearly. They have not been able to see their need for my Son and me. But soon the time will be here when a great work will begin. I will pour out my spirit. The seeds that have been planted will be harvested. I will bless and honour the prayers that have been raised by the intercessors. Tell them to continue earnestly without ceasing. My heart cries out for the lost sheep, my desire is that none should perish. These people are my people. Everyone, including every race and creed were ordained to be mine. My heart is in anguish when I see how so many of my people are shunned and ridiculed. Love them my daughter, reach out to them. Let my Son be seen through you.

"Tell the church in Thornhill to press into me for nothing will be accomplished without My hand in it. Many great and wonderful things will be seen, but unity and prayer must be the understanding for all the church. This new church is only the beginning. Set your sights on the heavenlies. Satan will not prevail, for I am Jehovah and I will win! I have won! Jesus my precious Son paid the price at Calvary. It is finished! Consider the victory! Do not despair, for you will move forward and see many come out of the miry pit, and it will happen in such a way that you will know that I AM at work!"

I was so totally awestruck by this vision that I could hardly contain myself. I shared it with Dale and with our small church and I shared it at the Airport Vineyard Christian Fellowship the following Sunday morning. Everyone seemed excited about what God had spoken through this vision. The North of Toronto

Intercessors were also excited to hear that God had been listening to the prayers that they had been raising to him since their conception the year before.

It is interesting to note that approximately three months later on January 20, 1994, the renewal known as The Toronto Blessing broke out at The Toronto Airport Vineyard Christian Fellowship, and we were able to witness the first fruits of this incredible time of renewal that I believe with all my heart is turning into the greatest revival the world has ever seen.

VISION CONFIRMED IN ARGENTINA

In November of 1993, Dale and I and John and Carol Arnott were able to attend a wonderful conference in Argentina with Ed Silvosa, Cindy Jacobs and C. Peter Wagner. It was in Argentina that I witnessed for the first time in my life the real meaning of revival. They had been experiencing revival for approximately 10 years and had seen their churches grow to 250,000 people.

We heard several excellent speakers talk about how we can strategically take our cities for God through repentance, spiritual mapping, intercession, and unity between denominations. We were so excited about what God had been doing in Argentina that it gave us hope for what He could do back home.

John Arnott was prayed for by Claudio Friesen, who had an amazing anointing to minister renewal to thousands at meetings throughout the world. John came back from Argentina a new man. God imparted vision to him that he could have a church of 100,000 with meetings going seven days a week, 24 hours a day.

CHAPTER 19

I WILL CHANGE
YOUR NAME

*Let love and faithfulness never leave you; bind them around
your neck, write them on the tablet of your heart. Then you will
win favor and a good name in the sight of God and man.*
Prov 3:3-4

For the first six months after I quit work, I missed my job terribly. If I did not think about it during the day, I dreamt about it at night. I asked God to show me what I was supposed to do for Him now that I had quit working and he kept telling me to "rest". For a girl who had always been performance oriented and somewhat of a workaholic, I found the concept of resting very difficult to comprehend.

I was helping Dale with the ongoing work of the church, but God had given me several prophetic words in the past that I would be used to bind up the brokenhearted and set the captives free. He had specifically said that I would go to the nations with a message of hope that would bring healing to many.

Summer time came once again — the summer of 1994 — and once again God did something dramatic in my life at Vineyard summer camp. By this time, the renewal was in full swing and I had been enjoying some incredible times with the Lord, but I still felt that there was something stopping me from being released into the ministry that He had spoken to me so many times.

One night, I was sitting in one of the meetings trying to listen to the speaker, but my mind was in a different place. I started to pray and I asked God, "Why, Lord, have I not been released into what you have been calling me to do. You told me that you wanted me to share my testimony of your goodness and mercy to the nations. Is there anything that I am doing or that I have done that is hindering your working through me?"

I waited for a brief moment and then I heard His still small voice say to me "Your name is written in my Lamb's Book of Life as 'Linda Diane'". It was then that this deep conviction hit me like a ton of bricks in my gut. The Lord convicted me of the time when I was a teenager and I had in a very rebellious attitude changed my name from Linda to Lynn. I had changed it to Lynn because there was a girl in my class who was popular and I wanted to be like her. In a sense, what I was saying to God was that I did not like whom He had made me and I wanted to be someone different. God showed me that I was in rebellion and that I was to change my name back to Linda.

That very night, I told Dale what the Lord had said to me and I chose to change it back to Linda. It was difficult getting use to at first, especially for friends who had only known me as Lynn, but in many ways it was very freeing. I phoned my Mother when I got home from camp and asked her to forgive me for changing the name that she had given me at birth.

I am always in awe of what God will do in our lives when we are willing to submit to His will. Because I had walked in so much rebellion, I had to learn some hard lessons and I was slowly realizing that Gods ways were best for my life.

Within a very short period of time God started opening doors for Dale and I to travel to different nations. We were in Finland three times within a year teaching conferences on "The Father Heart of God and "God's Grace in Brokenness" and in Hawaii three times that year teaching the same type of conferences.

The three trips that we made to Finland in 1996 were particularly significant. The first time we went, we were with our friend Marc Dupont. It was right in the midst of renewal and I was experiencing the holy laughter almost on an ongoing basis. Dale and I were with Marc to help with the ministry times and to share testimonies every session before he spoke. All week long God kept telling me that he wanted me to share His testimony. When I would share this with Dale he would say that the conference wasn't about brokenness, it was about renewal and so I would back off. As the week progressed the Lord's prompting got stronger. On Sunday morning we were sitting on the platform during worship and the Spirit of God came on me. I started to cry as I looked out over the six thousand people that were sitting in the auditorium. God spoke to me once again and said, "Linda I want you to share your testimony". I said, "but Lord I was going to share on joy," He said," How can they know me as a God of joy if they do not know me as a God of mercy and love." So I turned to Dale with tears streaming down my cheeks and told him that I was going to share my testimony. He agreed. When I was finished speaking, you couldn't hear a pin drop in the whole place. Marc got up to share and said that he was speechless. He had not heard the part of my story regarding the abortion. He stated that he and I had not collaborated on what he was going to speak on that morning, but it was exactly what I had talked about- the love and mercy of the Father Heart of God. After Marc was finished speaking, Dale and I went down among the people to pray for them. We spent hours ministering to people who, for the first time in their lives, were able to share openly and honestly about sins that they had never revealed to another living soul. The freedom and healing that took place that day was phenomenal. It is amazing what God will do when we walk in obedience.

On another occasion the Toronto Airport Vineyard were having a Grace and Love Conference with Terry Virgo and several other world famous speakers. My friend Carol Arnott was to be the host of the conference. On Sunday mornings, when I would do the announcements at our church about this conference coming up, the Lord said to me that He wanted me to share His testimony at that conference. I kept ignoring the prompting, which went on for three Sundays in a row. Finally I said to God, "Lord if you want me to speak at this conference then you are going to have to get Carol Arnott to call me". We hadn't talked in a very long time because we were all so busy with renewal. I felt that it would be too arrogant of me to call and invite myself to speak at a conference that was already booked and was to start in one week's time. Sure enough, the next day I got home from work to a telephone message from Carol who called just to find out how I was doing. Needless to say God worked it out for me to share His testimony at that conference and there were many people who came up to me afterwards who shared that their lives had been transformed by the story of Gods grace and mercy in my life.

TAKE THE LOG OUT OF YOUR OWN LIP:

This is a funny personal story that I had to include in this book about my wonderful romantic hubby Dale. A couple of years after we were married Dale and I and a group for people from our church went to a conference in the US. When we left a local eatery, Dale picked up one of the large toothpicks and started rolling it around in his mouth. When we got back to the hotel room he suddenly decided that he wanted to give me a romantic "Romeo kiss". He proceeded to fling me across his arms and plant a passionate kiss on my lips. I noticed that he still had the toothpick in his mouth and I wondered to myself, " what is he going to do with that sharp toothpick?" He was thinking that he would pull the toothpick back into his mouth before he planted the kiss on my lips. Well, he lost his footing and we landed on the bed. The very large and very sharp toothpick impaled my upper lip and struck me on the front tooth. My eyes filled with tears (it was very painful) but the look of horror on Dales face quickly made me forgive his wild act of chivalry. I got up, went into the bathroom and carefully pulled that toothpick from my lip. Our friends from church heard the commotion and soon everyone at the conference heard the news about Dale's romantic endeavours. They started to tease us, making comments like, "take the log out of your own lip", and talk about a "holy kiss" and "lip stick". Needless to say I have stayed clear of Dale whenever I see him with a toothpick in his mouth.

MY DIVINE APPOINTMENT WITH DEVLIN.

A few years ago Dale, Jeff and I went to a Canadian Vineyard Conference in Vancouver, British Columbia. While we were there, we visited Dale's son Jason who was living in Vancouver at the time. During the conference John Wimber was speaking on evangelism being the roots of the Vineyard and the importance for praying for a spirit of evangelism to help us with this. I went forward for prayer and received an anointing for evangelism. All week long I was having fun telling people that Jesus loved them. I prayed for three days that God would set up a divine appointment for me.

One evening we decided to go to the show. When we arrived at the theatre we discovered that we were an hour early, so we went to a nearby park to relax. Just as we entered the park I thought I heard the Lord tell me to look to the left. When I did, I saw a redheaded girl sitting in front of a fountain. The Lord told me to go over and talk to her. I told Dale what I thought God had said to me and that I was too scared to go.. He said, "come on I'll go with you", so we went over and introduced ourselves and then Dale and Jeff left me sitting alone with her. I cried out to God, "what do you want me to say to her Lord?" He said, "I will lead and guide you, I will give you the words". I found out that her name was Devlin and that she was seventeen years old. I commented that she seemed upset about something and discovered that she had just had a fight with her parents and had run away from home. I talked with her a little about my own upbringing and then asked her if she knew anything about Jesus. She said that she knew that we celebrated Christmas because of Him but had no formal church background. Over the next twenty minutes I shared the gospel with her in very simple terminology. I told her that if she had been the only person on earth that Jesus would have come to earth and died on the cross so that she could be saved from her sins and have abundant life. I could really sense the Holy Spirit there with us. Then I asked her if she would like to ask Jesus to come into her heart and make Him her Lord and Saviour. With a big smile on her face she said, "yes". Well I almost fell off the step and then proceeded to walk her through the "Romans road" to make sure she knew what she was about to do. She seemed to understand it clearly and so I led her in a salvation prayer. After-wards I asked the Holy Spirit to come and fill her and we both cried. Then I shared some practical things with her, like finding a Bible and where to start reading it, and how to find a church. The last thing I said to her was, "Devlin, I think God wants you to go home and forgive your parents" and she agreed. With that I got up and ran up the stairs to find Dale and Jeff. I can't ever remember in my life having such a high. I swung Jeff around and we laughed and I kept telling them what had happened. Then Dale, being a typical Pastor, wanted to know if I had given Devlin a phone number of one of the local Vineyards, so we went back down to find her but she had already left. I knew then that she had gone home to see her parents. I continue to pray for Devlin and I thank God for the way He honours our prayers for divine appointments. After all, it is His heart, "that none should perish but that all should come to eternal life".

CHAPTER 20

RENOUNCING CONTROL

But our citizenship is in heaven. And we eagerly await a Savior from there, the Lord Jesus Christ, who, by the power that enables him to bring everything under his control, will transform our lowly bodies so that they will be like his glorious body.
Phil 3:20-21

Through the years of our married life together, God allowed us to learn how to blend our families together. At times it was wonderful, but we also experienced our fair share of trials. God "never promised us a rose garden".

When Dale and I first met, our oldest boys were 13 years old and starting into the rebellious teenage years. Little did we know how well Chad and Jason would get along and how much they would walk away from things of God as the enemy used them to join forces together. Chad went from being a grade A student and what some people would call a "nerd", to failing in school, smoking cigarettes, and quitting school.

IN THE LIGHT OF GOD'S LOVE

When Chad was 16, he put what I thought were some pretty demonic posters up in his room. I would constantly tell him to take the posters down because they "slimed me". The Lord would tell me to leave Chad alone and stop speaking into his life, but I felt it was my motherly duty to make him do what I thought was right; so I kept harping at him.

At the same time I was very upset about a situation that was happening in our leadership team. I felt that I was not being heard on a certain issue that I felt I was right on.

We were in the process of holding our first conference called "The Father Loves You" with Ed Piorec from California and I knew that my heart was not right with God. I decided to go and get some counseling from our friends Ken and Lorraine Reeves. I shared with them all my frustrations about Chad and the posters and this other situation about not being heard.

They listened and let me cry. Then they told me that I had to renounce control of my right to speak into Chad's life and my right to be right in this other situation in leadership. Boy was I upset! I thought that they would have all kinds of empathy for me; instead, they were telling me that I had to let go of everything that I felt was important to me.

Well, I prayed the prayer of renouncement. I asked God to forgive me for trying to control Chad and for claiming my right to be right and I chose to let go and renounce control of Chad and the posters and my right to be heard on the leadership issue. Afterwards, I felt like a million pounds had been lifted off my shoulders. The first thing I noticed when I got home was that the posters no longer slimed me when I went into Chad's room.

Two weeks later, I went into his room one morning to wake him up for school. He sat bolt upright in bed (very unusual for him!), and said, "Do you notice anything different about my room?"

I looked around and saw that all of his posters were gone. "Chad, you took your posters down."

"Yah Mom, the Lord told me at 1 a.m. this morning to take them
down and burn them."

"Did He have to tell you twice?" I enquired. (I always had to
tell him twice about anything.) "Yes, Mom, He had to tell me
twice, and then I took them down and burned them in the fire
place."

I was so thrilled and surprised, but I knew the hand of God
was working. It is amazing to see God move — once we stop trying to have our way.

Another wonderful thing happened when Ed Piorec from
California came up to our church to do the "Father Loves You
conference". He brought with him a prophetic man named, Bob
Tremonte.

At one of the meetings Bob came over to me and said, "I
have a word from the Lord for you." I fell under the power of the
Spirit right beside one of the people in our leadership team who
was involved with the issue that I had prayed about. The Lord,
spoke into the situation through Bob and said that he had seen my
frustration, and that I was not being heard and that I had been
right about what we had been disagreeing about. The other person and myself started laughing and we were able to go to the
third person and resolve the issue. God will come to our defense
when we chose to take our hands off and let Him be God.

RENOUNCING CONTROL OF JEFFREY

From the time John and I had split up, he constantly asked
Jeffrey to come and live with him. It was understandable in some
ways, for I am sure that John must have really missed him.
However, it was very hard on the heart of a little boy. I remember him crying so often when he would come back from a visit
with his Dad. He would say to me, "Mom, when I get older I
want to go and live with Daddy". I would tell him, "Jeffy, when
you turn twelve years old and if you still feel that you want to live

with your Dad, then I will let you go". Dale and I had a great relationship with Jeff, but I knew that it was very important for him to be with his father. I did not want him to resent me when he became a man if I stopped him from going. I knew that my relationship with him would be more important long term. However, nothing prepared my heart for how painful his leaving would be for me. When he was twelve he left our home in Thornhill and moved to Owen Sound. For the first six months I cried everyday. I would journal and ask God why He had allowed so much pain in my life. I saw Jeff as a gift from God and now I only could see him every second weekend. After a year, I felt the Lord say to me that my time of grieving was over. Within a couple of weeks, Jeff decided to come back home to us. He was home with us for another year, but discovered that they did not have football as an extra-curricular sport at his high-school. Once again he returned to Owen Sound to live with his Dad, but this time the Lord had prepared my heart and I had been able to renounce control of Jeff and bless his life choices. I will always be thankful to God for my two wonderful sons.

CHAPTER 21

THE THORNHILL VINEYARD BEGINS

"Forget the former things; do not dwell on the past.
See, I am doing a new thing! Now it springs up;
do you not perceive it? I am making a way in the
desert and streams in the wasteland.
Isa 43:18-19

In May of 1992, Dale and I and our children had moved from Cambridge to the Thornhill area and began to develop a strategy for planting a new church in a primarily Jewish neighborhood. Dale was still working at the Airport Vineyard and I had just started my job at The Wexford (my job from heaven). During this time I took several courses and attended many conferences and eventually earned my ordination through The Association of Canadian Vineyards.

God initially told us that He would raise up 100 intercessors to pray for our new church plant as well as for the other churches in our area and for the lost. Dennis and Elizabeth Jones headed up the intercessory prayer project, which we called "The Kneeling

Army". They also were our first elders.

God started to pull many wonderful leaders together at that time; and, before long, we had a great worship team led by Ken and Marcia Meyer. Ken and Lorraine Reeves came on board as elders as well as leaders of our Prayer and Counseling Ministry. We began meeting weekly in small groups and we held occasional monthly celebrations.

In September of 1993, we and thirty other people were released with John and Carol Arnott's blessing to plant a church in Thornhill. On January 20, 1994, the "Toronto Blessing" began and 15 of the 30 people who came with us decided to return to the Airport — and who could blame them? Dale called it, "church planting in reverse". However, God was blessing us in many incredible ways. I was experiencing all kinds of crazy manifestations. I would laugh uncontrollably throughout our services. They were wonderful times of knowing the depths of God's love and the fruit of it was that I was being healed and loved back to life by the Lord.

Our church eventually grew to become a close-knit, loving family, which has been a source of great encouragement and love to Dale and me. It has not been without its problems and hurts, but we are so thankful to God that He has placed us in this community. God has given us a heart-felt love for the Jewish people and we have come to know some wonderful Messianic believers in this community.

It still amazes me how God can use a couple of broken people like Dale and I to bring healing and comfort to others. We have been truly thankful for the gift of healing and wholeness that He has brought to us through the trials that He has allowed in our lives.

At the time of this writing, The Thornhill Vineyard has been in existence almost ten years. We have moved to several different locations over the years and are presently situated in a lovely retail complex at 7775 Yonge St. The Lord gave me a vision for a place in the heart of the community which would be a refuge for the broken and downtrodden. A place where people could come and meet and feel loved and accepted. He said that it would be in the marketplace so that we would be easily accessible. God said that we would draw people from various nationalities and that we would be able to reach Jewish people who would come to buy at our store.

Families Unlimited is a Christian Resource Center which caters to the needs of our community in various different ways. We sell new books, music, videos, crafts, angels, bibles, and a wide assortment of gift items for confirmation, communion, baptism, and weddings. We also house a comfortable fireside lounge, tea-room, library and we were selling used clothing for $1.00 a pound. We have seen many people come through our doors who have been blessed by a much-needed prayer, a loving word of consolation or just a warm hug and a cup of tea. We provide free clothing and food to the homeless and have taken strangers into our home on occasion. Another service of Families Unlimited is to offer workshops and seminars to the community relating to felt needs and family issues. These include; Raising Kids Gods Way, Divorce Recovery, Blending Families, True Colors Personality Profiling and Alpha Courses. Our church services are also held in our building on Yonge St. We have a very family oriented congregation and always have a meal together after our 10:30 morning service.

Dale and I have been very happily married for more than eleven years. God chose the perfect man for me. It is so refreshing to be married to a strong spiritual leader who is not threatened by my calling or gifting from God. We are truly life partners who love and respect each other. This is not to say that we have not had our arguments over the years but we have learned to agree to disagree on certain issues and to become much more flexible in those things which are important to us. Our hearts cry is to help people who are struggling in their marriages to work things out. We have experienced first-hand the pain of divorce and the joy that walking in God's will can bring.

One of the areas that was a real struggle for me in our marriage is the concept of living in community. For almost the first eight years of our marriage we shared our home with others. Throughout this time I really did not enjoy it very much. I guess it was all about dying to self. God has allowed me to see my own selfish heart in these times and He has gradually changed my heart so that I now really enjoy living in Christian community. God has blessed us with a large home and we now have six other adults (who are not apart of our biological family) living under the same roof with us. Of course it is not without its problems and issues but all in all we are learning what God means when He says that we are to lay down our lives for our friends.

Even though it was very hard for me to give up my other step-children, God has blessed me with two other lovely children, Jason who is twenty-five and Anna who is twenty-four. Anna is presently finishing her Masters degree in International Development. Chad and Jason have been good friends since they met and they live together. Although they are not following the Lord at this time, Dale and I believe that one-day the promises that God has spoken to us about them will come to pass. Please pray for them. Jeff is a lovely sixteen-year old who lives with his father at the present time. We have a great relationship with him and miss him terribly because we only get to see him on weekends. Jeff is gifted in so many ways. He excels at sports and he recently tried out for the Canadian Idol competition for singing. His zest for life is contagious. God really does take the things that Satan intends for bad and turn them into something great. He is my special gift from God.

Since the time The Lord asked me to share His testimony and to take my story to the nations we have traveled to many places throughout the world. What a joy it has been to watch the Lord honour His promise to me as He heals and redeems the broken and devastated people of the world

We are so thankful to God for what He is doing in and through our lives. Who would have thought that a little girl from Cabbagetown would end up an ordained minister for the gospel of Jesus Christ? To God be the glory for the great things He has done.

PART V

WALKING OUT OF BROKENNESS INTO WHOLENESS

WALKING OUT OF BROKENNESS INTO WHOLENESS

I wanted to end this book with some practical steps that God used to help me walk out of brokenness into wholeness.

Each person, in one form or another, experiences some kind of brokenness in their lives, but it is how we respond to those difficulties that will determine whether we become broken in the right place or the wrong place. People broken in the wrong place often become bitter, angry and unforgiving, and are unable to develop healthy relationships with other people. They are unyielding to the will of God in their lives and often end up on a roller coaster of emotional pain and addictive life patterns. On the other hand, people broken in the right place become tender-hearted and yielded towards God. They are able to embrace their pain and come to learn by the mistakes they have made. They choose to forgive and let things go and as a result they become better as they allow God to mold and shape them into the people He intended them to be.

STEPS TO HEALING:

1. First and foremost we must come to a place of recognizing that without God we can do nothing. Phil 4:13: "I can do everything through him who gives me strength." We must understand that, if anything good is going to happen in us and through us, it will only come through our total trust and reliance on Christ in us to do the work. Our Christian walk should be one of resting and trusting, not striving and worrying.

2. We must desire healing more that anything else. Many people today are comfortable in the mind-set of being a victim and often do not know what they "would be" if they were healed up. God is more than willing to bring us to a place of healing but we have to take that first step of faith to earnestly seek it. God knows our hearts and it is the enemy who wants to hold us back and tell us the lie that we can never be set free or that we are not worthy of it. Do not believe that deceiver for a moment! One of the best books I have read on Inner Healing is Transformation of the Inner Man by John and Paula Sandford. I would highly recommend you to read this book and apply the biblical principles in it to your life. Seek out godly counselors who are equipped to help you in the process of being healed. I will expand on the teachings of the Sandfords that were particularly helpful to me later in this chapter.

3. The next step is choosing to walk in daily repentance and forgiveness. God commands in Matthew 6:14: "For if you forgive men when they sin against you, your heavenly Father will also forgive you." Matthew 6:15: "But if you do not forgive men their sins, your Father will not forgive your sins."

WALKING OUT OF
BROKENNESS INTO WHOLENESS

If we are ever going to walk in a state of wholeness and holiness with God, we need to keep short accounts before God regarding our own sin, but we must also be willing to forgive those who hurt us. (Further teaching on forgiveness will be unwrapped later in this chapter)

4. Choosing to renounce control of those things that we hold on to so desperately is the next step in walking out your healing. You may recall how I had to renounce control of certain issues in my life before God could speak into them and have His way. God wants us to give over every aspect of our lives to Him everyday. It is only then that we can truly rest in the knowledge that He has everything in control and only wants the best for us. It is all part of the dying process as described in Gal 2:20 " I have been crucified with Christ and I no longer live, but Christ lives in me. The life I live in the body, I live by faith in the Son of God, who loved me and gave himself for me." We need to die to self so that our will is in line with the will of God for our lives. My husband Dale often says, "First we have to get saved from our sin, then we have to get saved from ourselves", and "The only good Christian is a dead Christian"- that is dead to sin and alive to God. For us, Christianity is a lifestyle worth dying for.

5. Desire to seek His face and hear His voice every day. Knowing the Fathers love for me has been one of the most-life changing and healing things that has happened to transform me. The more time you spend with "Abba Daddy" the more you will understand at a heart level how much you are loved and cherished. People can say many kind things to you, but when the Father speaks into a situation that you are struggling with, He settles the issue. Throughout our lifetime Satan speaks many lies to us about ourselves through other

121

people Try to spend time every day journaling. Studying Mark Virklers book, "Communion With God" enabled me to understand the difference between hearing Satan's voice, my thoughts and God's voice. Virkler encourages the reader to take time every day to write down in a journal what we feel God is saying to us. To start off with, ask God to tell you what He thinks of you. I know that you will be amazed at what He will speak to you. It might even make you blush.

6. Be willing to share your brokenness with others. We read in the following passage that we are to comfort others with the comfort that we have received. 2 Cor. 1:3-5: "Praise be to the God and Father of our Lord Jesus Christ, the Father of compassion and the God of all comfort who comforts us in all our troubles, so that we can comfort those in any trouble with the comfort we ourselves have received from God. For just as the sufferings of Christ flow over into our lives, so also through Christ our comfort overflows." A couple of years ago I had a dream which I believe God was using to teach me the importance of being transparent with people and with Him. In the dream, Dale and I went to a house where many of our friends from The Thornhill Vineyard were having a party. We were all dancing and worshipping God. Suddenly I took off all of my clothes and started dancing before the Lord (this was in the dream, remember). Some of the people saw me and encouraged what I was doing, (including my husband). Others didn't even seem to notice that I was naked. A small group of people were horrified and one of my girlfriends brought me a white terry cloth bathrobe and suggested that I put it on. I put the robe on, but immediately noticed that it hindered my ability to worship, and so I took it off. When I first woke up I was horrified and shared it with Dale. (He

thought the dream was funny but saw the significance in it right away. When I journalled about it, the Lord showed me that He is blessed by my transparency and that the white robe signified a spirit of religion that often hinders us from being open and honest with others and God. When the Lord asked me to share my testimony about the abortion He promised me that He would not only bring healing to the nations, but that He would bring healing to me. He has been faithful. One example of this is that God used my testimony to bring my husband's ex-wife back to Him, when she was at a place of believing that God could never forgive her for walking away from Him and walking in sin. He has restored her to Himself.

Walk out your healing! We are called to walk by faith, not by sight. Each day brings its joys as well as its trials. None of us are exempt from experiencing trials and tribulations. God would have us claim the victory that we have for healing in Christ Jesus and believe that by His stripes we are healed. We are not called to be victims, but victors. Too many people I have met over the years are comfortable in their "victimization" and don't want to walk into wholeness because they feel that they won't know who they are. God's heart is that His love can break the bondage's and provide us with a life that will glorify Him

Read His word! Study it, meditate on it, devour it, own it. God longs to speak a "rema", life - giving word to you. The more you memorize scripture, the more you bury it in your heart, the more it will help you through your daily life experiences. He will lead and guide you into all truth as you seek His face and learn what His will is for your life. Psa 119:11 "I have hidden your word in my heart that I might not sin against you."

THE POWER OF FORGIVENESS

What is forgiveness? The unnatural ability to let go and not hold people accountable for the hurts, injustices and harms that they have purposely or non-purposely brought to our lives. Forgiveness is the act and attitude towards those who have wronged us, which restores relationship and fellowship.

Forgiveness is the most powerful, important, and joyous message the Gospel of the Lord Jesus Christ brings to us!

FORGIVENESS IS:

Extending undeserved mercy

Letting go of the offence

Not expecting an apology

A Christian lifestyle

A choice, a conscious effort

A risk-being vulnerable

Blessing those who persecute you

WHY FORGIVE?

Forgiveness is the antidote to sin: Forgiveness reunites us with God, brings us into unity with others and restores our integrity. If we are to be healthy, happy individuals, forgiveness is not an option, it is necessary.

2. God commands us to forgive: The Amplified Version of the Bible best describes forgiveness:

"For if you forgive people their trespasses, that is, their reckless and willful sins, letting them go and giving up resentment, your heavenly Father will also forgive you. But, if you do not forgive others their trespasses, their reckless and willful sins, leaving, letting them go and giving up resentment neither will your Father forgive your trespasses". Jesus, Amplified Bible

Withholding forgiveness keeps us under the power of the person who caused the wounding. John 20:23 Whose soever sins ye remit, they are remitted unto them; and whose soever sins ye retain, they are retained. (KJV) Forgiveness releases us from the power of the sin and from under the control of the perpetrator. It also frees our offender to receive God's grace and mercy as we pray for God to bless our enemies.

REASONS FOR UNFORGIVENESS:
Fear of being hurt again
The person isn't sorry
Ongoing bitterness
The offence was too great
The person keeps repeating the offence
I'm too angry to forgive
No one else will get even
I have tried but I can't or don't feel like it

RESULTS OF UNFORGIVENESS:
Ongoing instant replay-this is where you relive the event
   over and over in your mind
Ongoing health problems
Shortened life span
Inability to trust others
Constant conflict in relationships
Inability to love
Attack by Satan – unforgiveness is sin that gives the enemy
   the right to inflict you.
Inability to receive healing
Inability to walk in the Spirit- sin grieves the Holy Spirit

A life of unforgiveness is a life of bitterness and torment. It is a life, which opens the door to all kinds of demonic oppression such as addiction, compulsive behaviours, and depression. It often can be a life of unrest and violence.

ACHIEVING FORGIVENESS:

Honestly desire to become free of the burden of unforgiveness and prepare to forgive.

Sit down with a fair-minded counselor or friend and talk over the situation with them.

Pray specifically about the person or situation that is a focus of unforgiveness and ask for forgiveness for reactions that you have had towards the person who has hurt you. Verbally chose to forgive the person(s) who have offended you.

Do something to bless the person who has offended you (if possible) Rom. 12:20-21 "On the contrary: "If your enemy is hungry, feed him; if he is thirsty, give him something to drink. In doing this, you will heap burning coals on his head." Do not be overcome by evil, but overcome evil with good."

Be prepared to suffer hurt to fulfill God's purpose. 1 Pet 3:15-17 But in your hearts set apart Christ as Lord. Always be prepared to give an answer to everyone who asks you to give the reason for the hope that you have. But do this with gentleness and respect, keeping a clear conscience, so that those who speak maliciously against your good behavior in Christ may be ashamed of their slander. It is better, if it is God's will, to suffer for doing good than for doing evil.

Seek Reconciliation: Mat 5:23 -24 "Therefore, if you are offering your gift at the altar and there remember that your brother has something against you, leave your gift there in front of the altar. First go and be reconciled to your brother; then come and offer your gift.

WHERE IS THE POWER IN FORGIVENESS?

Reconciliation with God and man.

Blessing- Inner healing and deliverance

Stops reaping of generational wounding and sin.

Releases the resurrection power of Christ's spirit in us.

Understanding the Father's great love for us.

TEACHINGS FROM JOHN AND PAULA SANDFORD

During the first six months after I started attending The Cambridge Vineyard, God took me on a fast paced radical journey of inner healing and deliverance. Previously I had been discouraged to look into these truths and was totally amazed to find out how much they affected my whole life and have since brought me into so much freedom.

The following information is an overview of what I learned about myself and those keys that were helpful in setting me free. The teachings helped me to discover why I did what I did and how I had reaped the consequences of so many sins in my life.

THE SCRIPTURAL LAWS:

1. Honoring Parents: Eph 6:2-3 "Honor your father and mother"—which is the first commandment with a promise—"that it may go well with you and that you may enjoy long life on the earth." One of the most important commandments that radically effected my whole life is this one. We are called to honor, obey and respect our parents, whether or not their behaviour deserves it. We will be held accountable before God regarding our reactions towards them. In my case I judged my Father in my heart for not being loving and affectionate, for not wanting to bless me financially and for his drinking and attitude towards my Mom.

There are some situations in which children grow up in homes of totally abusive parents, i.e. sexual or physical abuse. I think it would be almost impossible to not dislike or dishonor a parent in that case. However, each of us is responsible before God if we hold anger, hatred or unforgiveness towards our parents. If you want to walk away from the re-occurring pain and ongoing difficulties in your life, it is best to ask God to forgive you for any reactions that you have had toward your parents and chose to forgive them of the offences they caused or continue to cause you.

2. Judging with Impure Hearts and Becoming what we Judge

Mat 7:1-2 *"Do not judge, or you too will be judged. For in the same way you judge others, you will be judged, and with the measure you use, it will be measured to you. Rom 2:1 You, therefore, have no excuse, you who pass judgment on someone else, for at whatever point you judge the other, you are condemning yourself, because you who pass judgment do the same things.* These scriptures focus on judging others with impure hearts, with an attitude of blame, condemnation or self-righteousness. It is not wrong to look at a sin, such as abortion, and believe it to be "the killing of an unborn child". However it is wrong to judge others as I did, with people who were divorced, women who had abortions, and my father who drank too much. I ended up living out all of the things that I had judged. My first husband was very much like my father. I ended up divorced twice, something that I would never have wanted from life. I chose to murder my unborn child, something that I had self-righteously judged as a nurse when I refused to look after women who had abortions. Thank God I have been able to understand these Biblical truths and repent for my judgmental attitude

3. Reaping and Sowing: *Gal 6:7-8 Do not be deceived: God cannot be mocked. A man reaps what he sows. The one who sows to please his sinful nature, from that nature will reap destruction; the one who sows to please the Spirit, from the Spirit will reap eternal life.* I believe that every good deed sows blessing and

will reap blessing and that every evil deed sows harm and will reap destruction of some kind. God revealed to me many ways in which I sowed negatively and have suffered the consequences. The Bible states that the reaping of our sins can be passed down to even the third and fourth generation unless they are repented of. . I am constantly checking myself in this area because it is important to keep a clean slate before God every day. I do not want any more negative reaping from the sins I have sown.

COMMON SINFUL PRACTICES THAT RESULT FROM BREAKING THESE SCRIPTURAL LAWS:

Bitter Root Judgement: *1 Cor 4:5 Therefore judge nothing before the appointed time; wait till the Lord comes. He will bring to light what is hidden in darkness and will expose the motives of men's hearts. At that time each will receive his praise from God.*

This practice operates under both the laws of judging and reaping and sowing. We will either become what we judge or we will reap the consequences of the judgement.

Bitter Root Expectations: *Heb 12:15 See to it that no one misses the grace of God and that no bitter root grows up to cause trouble and defile many.* I had many bitter root expectations in my life. The words that we speak out of our mouth can be self-fulfilling prophecy and Satan will use them against you. Often when you expect things to go wrong, they will.

Parental Inversion: *Col 3:21 Fathers, do not embitter your children, or they will become discouraged.* This sinful practice often occurs when one or more parents are either absent from the home or immature or sinful. An older child may end up having to take on the role of the other parent in order to help with the responsibilities around the house. The parent will share things with the child that may be totally inappropriate for his level of maturity. As a result, a person raised in a home with parental inversion will usually either become over responsible adults, or they may go the other way and revert to a more immature state. Some of the symptoms of such a person may include not being able to trust authority figures or the Lordship of Jesus. They may have a hard time receiving nurture and love from primary people in their lives. They won't be able to enjoy life and just have fun. A person having grown up in such an atmosphere needs to ask God to reveal to them any judging that they may have made towards their parents and to ask forgiveness for their reactions. Freedom will come when they have truly been able to forgive their parents at a heart level.

Inner Vows: *Prov 20:25 It is a trap for a man to dedicate something rashly and only later to consider his vows.* Inner vows are determinations that we often make when we are children that become "computer programs" within our nature. Even though they may be made as children and often forgotten, they have more power by virtue of their hiddenness. I made many vows over my young life, such as-I never want to have a colicky baby or a caesarean section and I ended up having both. When I woke up on the recovery room table after having my first son Chad I was in excruciating pain. My husband came in all excited to tell me that we had a beautiful baby boy. The first words out of my mouth were," good, I wouldn't want to bring a girl into this mans world". (I had a bad attitude at that time about male- female roles). I believe that the words I spoke cursed my womb and that years later when I had two miscarriages they were little girl babies that I wasn't able to bring into this world. Since I have repented I am sure that if I were still fertile that I would be able carry a female child to full term. I thank God that He has blessed me with a lovely stepdaughter.

Performance Orientation: Performance orientation occurs

in homes where stringent demands for behaviour have not been properly balanced with enough love and affection. We believe the lie that I am only loved if I can perform well enough to earn other peoples approval. At the heart of every person is fear, the fear of failure, rejection, not being accepted, or not being able to measure up to the standards of others. I was an extremely performance-oriented child. I lacked affection and attention from my father and tended to see my heavenly father as an extension of my Dad. My Mom was very loving and encouraging but I still yearned for my Daddy's approval. I have had much healing in this area over the past several years but God continues to bring healing as I learn to understand my value in Christ Jesus and not in what others think of me.

Spiritual Rebellion: The Sandfords define spiritual rebellion as being in a state of not liking the circumstances of our lives, i.e. who we are, how God made us, i.e. sex, physical appearance or the family we were raised in. I also was affected by this sinful practice because I did not like being female and I did not appreciate the name that my parents had given me. I use to complain to Mom, why did you call me Linda- it sounds so stupid. She would say, I liked it because it was musical. I also use to tease Mom that I inherited her bad nails, and the "Walton Spread" which was mom's way of defining her large backside. Of course I have repented of these things, as you read in the body of this book, and God has since brought tremendous healing in these areas. (I am now very thankful to be female and I still have the bad nails and large backside)

In conclusion, I would encourage everyone who is desiring healing for their lives to seek Gods will, to listen to His wonderful voice, to bathe in the light of His incredible love and walk in obedience. There is no better place to be than in the Light Of His Love.

Epilogue:

I have been so blessed over the years by the response of many of the people who have read my book. I am thankful that God has used the difficult experiences that I went through to help others understand that God is a loving, caring Father who forgives and redeems us. In the process of revising and reprinting my book I thought it would be beneficial for the reader to update you as to what has been happening in the ten years since my book was first published

In 2004, after Pastoring The Thornhill Vineyard for twelve years, Dale and I listened to a tape by Wesley Campbell detailing the plight of the 34 Million orphans in Africa and decided to take a trip to Malawi with an organization called Hope For The Nations. We came back totally blown away by the situation that we experienced there and vowed that we would like to do whatever we could to help alleviate some of the suffering that we had seen. We had been feeling for some time that God was going to bring about change in our lives but hadn't really understood what He had in mind for us. At first we did a fund raising project and were able to raise enough money to build an orphan home at the Hope Village in Malawi but we were frustrated because we knew that with our income we could not afford to make any real significant dent in the huge issues of injustice that we had witnessed in Africa.

After we returned from Africa my sister Debbie discovered a magnesium supplement called Natural Calm that significantly changed her life. She had been suffering with migraine headaches since the age of 12 and by the time she was 46 Debbie was experiencing an average of 3-4 migraines each week. She had tried every natural remedy known to man and was taking $500 worth of migraine pain medication a month that provided very little relief and a lot of side effects. She ordered the Natural Calm from the US

(Natural Calm is the top selling magnesium supplement in the USA) and within a month she went from 3-4 migraines a week to one a month. As I watched her get better and better I started to investigate the benefits of magnesium and decided to try to the product myself for insomnia, fibromyalgia and low bone density. The first night I took Natural Calm I slept better than I had slept in years and within the first week I got rid of 70% of the muscle pain.

Because I had worked with the Ministry of Health during my years as a Director of Nursing I called Health Canada to find out the process for importing Natural Health Products into Canada and immediately applied for a Product Number for Natural Calm. When Dale realized how successful the product was in the US he said that if we were willing to give all proceeds after expenses to the extreme poor then he would be willing to help me with the business and of course I agreed. In 2007 we stepped down from being Pastors and now spend the majority of our time promoting health with our magnesium supplements and sharing our wealth with the extreme poor.

At the time of this writing it is June 2010 and we have a line of Natural Health Products in over 1500 stores and wellness clinics across Canada. We are constantly amazed as to how God continues to bless and grow our business and to allow us to be a blessing in the marketplace as well as being able to help orphans in Africa. When we first went to Africa we were financing the building of orphanages, schools and water well drilling. We were working mainly in Kenya at that time and as we traveled around we discovered that the majority of people there were eating a very low nutrient diet consisting mainly of corn meal and rice. As a result of eating such poor diets the people have jeopardized immune systems so when they get an infection their bodies do not have the ability to fight it off and they will succumb to their illness. Dale spent a month at Manor House Agricultural School in Kenya to learn about Biointensive Organic Gardening. We decided that we wanted to start an organization-Organics 4 Orphans, which would help to train people in Africa to grow their own healthy foods that would provide food security, nutritional training, disease prevention and income generation. While Dale was training at the Agricultural College he was mentored by Boaz, one of the teachers at the college, and he decided that we would hire Boaz to be our first OAT (Organic Agricultural Trainer) for Organics 4 Orphans. We now have over 100 community groups in Kenya who are doing the Organics 4 Orphans protocol and we are branching out to the countries surrounding Kenya like Ethiopia and Uganda.

Our long term dream is to spend 3 months in Africa helping the extreme poor eat healthy nourishing food, enjoy our beloved family here in Canada and hopefully be able to experience some of the world's most beautiful places, sailing. Anna, our daughter married her sweetheart Tim in December 2004 and Jason continues working in construction and renovations. In 2009 we had the honor of performing the wedding ceremonies of both our sons. Chad and Michelle were married Sept 19th and Jeff and Tricia on Oct 17th. On April 17, 2010 we became grandparents for the first time to Chad's son Jackson. My 85 year old mother Jean moved in with us in April of 2009 and we are blessed to be able to care for her during her golden years.

I often sit back in amazement when I think of what God has done in our lives over the past 20 years since I met my significant wonderful husband Dale. How I thank God for the incredible opportunities that He has given us. Praise His holy name!